THE
EVERYTHING®
Harmonica Book

Dear Reader,

The diatonic harmonica is a beautiful instrument. Who would have thought that twenty little reeds housed in a compact little body could produce the glorious array of musical sounds, styles, techniques, and blazing masters that form the history of the harp over the last 150 years?

The harmonica is one of the most affordable instruments, and certainly one of the most portable. You can take it with you anywhere and practice whenever you have a free moment. The more you play with it, the faster your skills will grow, and your growing success will give you the energy to forge on to greater heights.

In this book you'll learn the terminology, or "language," of the harmonica so that you'll be able to talk knowledgeably to other harp players and understand what they say to you. You'll also learn the proper way to hold the harmonica, how to position your mouth to get the best sound, and the scales and chords you'll need to play your favorite songs. By the time you get to the end of the book you should be able to play complete songs by yourself and know how to play with other musicians as well.

We're honored that you've chosen *The Everything® Harmonica Book with CD* as your guide on this exciting journey. Now let's get going!

Douglas Lichterman
Blake Brocksmith
Gary Dorfman

Welcome to the EVERYTHING Series!

These handy, accessible books give you all you need to tackle a difficult project, gain a new hobby, comprehend a fascinating topic, prepare for an exam, or even brush up on something you learned back in school but have since forgotten.

You can choose to read an *Everything®* book from cover to cover or just pick out the information you want from our four useful boxes: e-questions, e-facts, e-alerts, e-ssentials. We give you everything you need to know on the subject, but throw in a lot of fun stuff along the way, too.

We now have more than 400 *Everything®* books in print, spanning such wide-ranging categories as weddings, pregnancy, cooking, music instruction, foreign language, crafts, pets, New Age, and so much more. When you're done reading them all, you can finally say you know *Everything®*!

QUESTIONS?
Answers to
common questions

FACTS
Important snippets
of information

ALERTS!
Urgent
warnings

Quick
handy tips

DIRECTOR OF INNOVATION Paula Munier

MANAGING EDITOR, EVERYTHING SERIES Lisa Laing

COPY CHIEF Casey Ebert

ACQUISITIONS EDITOR Lisa Laing

DEVELOPMENT EDITOR Brett Palana-Shanahan

EDITORIAL ASSISTANT Hillary Thompson

ILLUSTRATOR Mark DiVico

Visit the entire Everything® series at *www.everything.com*

THE
EVERYTHING®
HARMONICA
BOOK
with CD

Learn the basics and play your favorite songs

Douglas Lichterman, Blake Brocksmith,
and Gary Dorfman

avon, massachusetts

This book is dedicated to the great players, past and present, who
have made the harmonica the prominent instrument that it is today.

An Everything® Series Book.
Everything® and everything.com® are registered trademarks of F+W Publications, Inc.

Published by Adams Media, an F+W Publications Company
57 Littlefield Street, Avon, MA 02322 U.S.A.
www.adamsmedia.com

ISBN 10: 1-59869-482-0

ISBN 13: 978-1-59869-482-6

Printed in the United States of America.

J   I   H   G   F   E   D   C   B   A

Library of Congress Cataloging-in-Publication Data
is available from the publisher.

This book is available at quantity discounts for bulk purchases.
For information, please call 1-800-289-0963.

Contents

Acknowledgments

Thanks to my coauthors for their hard work and dedication; to Lisa Laing and everybody at Adams Media; to our agent, Bob Diforio; to Marc Schonbrun for his excellent collaboration on the tabs and scores; and to all the great harmonica players who have inspired us and driven us forward. Special thanks to my wife, Gabrielle—life is heaven here with you.

—DL

I would like to thank my coauthors for inviting me into this journey, and my wife, Tangerre, for putting up with me. I would also like to thank Brian Krammer and Vincent Messina for telling me to keep playing.

—BB

I would like to thank all the harmonica players in bands I've played in over the years who have inspired me to love and play this incredible instrument that I keep in my back pocket. Special thanks to my coauthors; to my band, BLUESOLE; and, of course, to my lovin' family, Isabelle, Jonathan, Evan, and my Mom for constantly understanding while I'm trying to nail those bends.

—GD

Top Ten Things You'll Learn From This Book

1. Straight harp—playing the major scales used for folk songs and traditional music.

2. Cross harp—playing blues scales and making the harmonica swing on rock and blues songs.

3. Reading harmonica tablature, the special musical notation just for the harmonica.

4. Understanding chord progressions and how to play over them.

5. Note bending techniques—the soul of your harmonica sound.

6. Exciting riffs, phrases, and vamps to impress your friends.

7. Playing by ear—how to figure out the key of the music you're listening to.

8. How to maximize your practice time by getting organized and building your techniques effectively.

9. Harmonica heroes—getting inspiration from the giants who have led the way to where harmonica music is today.

10. Equipment you'll need—microphones, amps, and effects to get the big harmonica sound.

Introduction

▶ WELCOME TO *The Everything® Harmonica Book with CD*! It's exciting that you've decided to develop your harmonica skills, and this book will guide you down the path to becoming a solid harp player. By getting this book and a harmonica, you've already taken the first step on your journey to being proficient on this wonderful instrument.

This book is intended for beginner to intermediate harmonica players. You don't have to know anything about harmonica to get started with this book, but even if you have been playing for a little while you'll find that this book contains plenty of useful information to improve your understanding, technique, and musicianship.

The harmonica's history in American culture is a rich and vibrant one. The instrument was an instant hit when first introduced here around the mid-1800s. Its portable size and rich, appealing sound made it a favorite of cowboys, soldiers, hobos, and just about anybody with a pocket.

The harmonica first appeared on the American music scene in blues and folk music, but it has since expanded into many other kinds of music including jazz, rock, country, and classical, and its sphere of musical genres is still growing. Sampled harmonica is showing up on Hip Hop and Techno albums. Wildly overdriven and distorted sounds you'd never believe could be produced by a harmonica are gracing tracks of some modern rock bands. Whatever style of music you want to play, there's a way to fit a harmonica into it.

One reason for the harmonica's wide appeal is that you can play it the first time you try. Even a child can get a nice sound out of a harmonica on the first attempt, and if you're just trying to pick out a melody in the major key the harmonica is in, it almost happens automatically for you because of the way the harmonica is tuned. But simple as the harmonica seems at first, it's also a complicated instrument, and there are a million things to learn before you really master it. Just listen to one Little Walter song if you have any doubt.

Another interesting social aspect of the harmonica is the way it affords musical opportunity to virtually everyone. Since its introduction, the harmonica has been an instrument of choice for people who didn't have the means for expensive instruments or music lessons at the conservatory. As such, it has connected a wide range of people to music on a personal level by providing a simple and accessible instrument to use as a voice for their expression.

Many of the great harmonica players have displayed a willful stubbornness about ensuring the viability of their instrument, taking the instrument's potential for expression well beyond what anyone thought possible by developing new techniques through their diligent play and practice. The harmonica may not be a Stradivarius violin or a Steinway piano—but can you carry those in your pocket?

To use this book you will need a diatonic harmonica in the key of C. If you don't already have one, here are some recommended instruments to choose from:

- Hohner "Marine Band" C harmonica
- Hohner "Special 20" C harmonica
- Lee Oskar C harmonica

Expect to pay about $20 to $30 for one of these harmonicas at a music store or from an online outlet.

Now it's your turn to enter the rich, vibrant, and electrifying world of harmonica music with *The Everything® Harmonica Book with CD* as your guide.

How to Use This Book and CD

To get the most out of this book, you should know about some of the notation and terms that will be used throughout this text. Some of it you may have seen before, and some of it may be new to you.

Standard Notation and Harmonica Tablature

For every instructional example that has an accompanying recorded track, there will be one line of standard notation written on the staff, and one line of harmonica tablature below it. Note that the harmonica tab by nature does not indicate rhythmic notation, so you'll have to use the standard notation and the recorded track itself to get that information. Harmonica tab only indicates which hole on the harmonica to play, whether it's a blow note or a draw note, and what kind of bend, if any, to use.

Harmonica Diagrams

Harmonica diagrams are used to illustrate the harmonica itself. The diagram is a front view of the harmonica, with the ten holes indicated and numbered. Hole 1 on the left side of the diagram has the lowest pitch notes, and hole 10 on the right side has the highest pitch notes.

Audio Examples

As often as possible, the examples are played on the accompanying audio CD that is included with this book. The examples are played for you so you can hear the concepts, play along with them, and use them to check yourself. In this book, the CD symbol with a track number underneath it corresponds to the track on the CD. Being able to hear audio examples of the exercises or riffs in the book is very helpful in speeding along your understanding and your progress on the harmonica.

CHAPTER 1

Let's Start

A good place to kick off your harmonica journey is to take a look at some of the different kinds of harmonicas that exist, with particular attention to the one that you'll be using in your studies. This chapter will also talk about what to look for when you buy a harmonica.

First Things First: Types of Harmonicas

Harmonicas come in a wide range of varieties, the majority of which have fallen out of common usage. The focus here will be on the ones that you're most likely to run across as you learn to play.

Diatonic Versus Chromatic

The diatonic harmonica is the most popular and the one most commonly used, since it has traditionally been an inexpensive and widely available instrument. It's by far the most often used instrument in blues, rock, country, and traditional folk music.

The diatonic harmonica has ten holes, each of which produces one note when blown and another note when drawn. The instrument has a basic range of nineteen notes, rather than twenty, because the 2-hole draw and the 3-hole blow notes are the same. Beyond that, many other notes can be produced on the harmonica using note-bending techniques. (More on note bending in Chapter 5.)

The diatonic harp does not contain every note of the scale—rather it is based on a pentatonic, or five-note, scale utilizing equal temperament tuning.

FACT

Equal temperament tuning is a system by which the octave is divided into twelve equal half steps. It was designed to help different types of instruments with different tuning systems be able to play together and sound in tune with each other. Most Western-scaled instruments use equal temperament tuning.

The chromatic harmonica is based on the full twelve-note scale, giving it more reeds and therefore more range. It also has a device for changing key, usually a plunger that blocks certain holes and reeds when depressed. The diatonic harmonica has no such device, so one must purchase different harps to play in different keys.

FIGURE 1-1: Blow notes and draw notes of a diatonic harmonica/chromatic example

TRACK 1   TAB: 1↑   2↑   3↑   4↑   5 ↑   6↑   7↑   8↑   9↑   10↑   Blow Notes

TAB: 1↓   2↓   3↓   4↓   5↓   6↓   7↓   8↓   9↓   10↓   Draw Notes

Chromatic

Other Types of Harmonicas

There are many other types of harmonicas, including:

- **Octave harmonicas:** These banana-shaped harmonicas have two holes stacked vertically for each note. The notes are tuned an octave apart, which gives the instrument a rich chorus sound similar to a twelve-string guitar.

- **Bass harmonicas:** These bad boys are about a foot and a half long! They have the standard ten holes (just a lot bigger) and take special breathing techniques to play because it takes so much air to move the big reeds. They were popular and used quite a bit in music from several decades ago, but are not in wide use today.

- **Miniature harmonicas:** At the other end of the spectrum are the miniatures. These teensy harps are manufactured to the same standards as their big brothers. They only have four holes and play in the high soprano range, but it's still possible to get good bends and trills on them, and although they're so tiny, their holes are almost as big as on a regular-size harp.

However, the two types that are most commonly used and have become most prominent in modern music are the diatonic and the chromatic harmonica. And the one that this book will concentrate on is the diatonic.

Different Keys: Highs and Lows

Diatonic harmonicas come in every key—C, D, E, F, G, A, and B, as well as in some of the half steps in between. The deepest-sounding normal-size diatonic harmonica is the G harp, and the highest sounding one is the F harp. Note that each of the keys will play slightly differently from the others. For example, the reeds will feel tighter on the higher-pitched harps and looser on the lower-pitched ones. This means that more air is required to play the lower-pitched harps. Also it will be harder to get certain bends to work on the higher-pitched harps.

The C harmonica is the recommended harp for beginners. Falling right in the middle of the pitch range of harmonicas, meaning that there are three harps with lower pitch (G, A, and B) and three with higher pitch (D, E, and F), the C harp does not present the challenges of using the lowest, and therefore loosest, or the highest and tightest reeds that exist. Rather it gives you a comfortable range of easy-to-use reeds. Another advantage is that the C harmonica plays in the keys of C and G, which are the keys of many commonly played folk songs. In addition, C harmonicas are the easiest to find in any store that sells musical instruments, whereas finding harps in the other keys can be tricky.

Harmonica Brand Names

The most common brand names in the United States are Hohner (by far the oldest and most established harmonica makers in the world), Lee Oskar, Yamaha, Huang, and Suzuki. The Marine Band is the most traditional of the Hohners and is a truly amazing instrument in the hands of those who can play. It was the "choice" of all of the early masters—because it was likely the only harmonica available at the time. Marine Band harps have a wooden comb.

QUESTION?

Is it true some old blues players used to dunk their harps in hard liquor?

Oral tradition tells of the great harp players soaking their harmonicas in booze before and during performance to make the comb expand and add to that "wet" sound, which might be attributed to the liquor lubricating the reeds and making them vibrate a little more widely. Little Walter Jacobs is credited as being the first to do this.

You are advised to start out with an established brand of harmonica such as Hohner or Lee Oskar, with Yamaha and Suzuki as next-tier choices.

If you notice that your harmonica is put together with nails instead of screws, you should move on to a different instrument. That's because if the plate comes off or if you want to take it off for repairs, it will never go on as tightly again.

Avoid toy harmonicas or harmonicas made of plastic, some of which even have plastic reeds. And avoid buying old or used harmonicas for the purpose of playing, although they do make great collectors items.

What Harmonica Should You Buy?

When buying a harmonica you should look for several things:

- Does it look sturdy?
- Do the reeds sound like they are tight? The reeds are attached with welds, and after a while metal fatigue will make them go out of tune and occasionally break. Loose reeds will have an audible buzzing sound.
- Are the top shield and bottom shield well sealed to the comb? If the shields are not sealed, then at best you will get a poor sound and at worst cut your lips while playing.

Most purveyors of fine harmonicas have a tester, which looks like a bellows and will be used to test your harp before you buy it. This is a very important step because variations in quality can occur during the manufacturing process. Even the conditions under which they have been shipped can make a difference. Occasionally a shipment of harmonicas with wooden combs will get dropped in water or be exposed to extreme moisture, which will cause the combs to expand and then contract. Look for an uneven surface where the comb either sticks out or is recessed from the line of the reed plates to know if this has occurred.

When the salesperson tests the harp in front of you, make sure they use a lot of air pressure to hear how the reeds sound under pressure. This will sometimes cause a stick in a reed, meaning that the reed will suddenly stop making sound—and you want to know that before you buy it. It's not necessarily a bad harp, just one that requires better breath control. This usually occurs with the higher-keyed harps like F and E. If this happens, ask your salesperson to test another harp for you.

The recommended harmonicas would be either the Hohner or the Lee Oskar brand. The Hohner Special 20s are a big favorite—they list for about $37 (but can be purchased online for $20) and last a long time under performance conditions. They also have a plastic comb, which helps to make them very reliable-sounding, as they are not subject to changing humidity levels in the air.

Maintenance and Repair

Maintaining your harps is simple. Rule number one—keep them clean! It's possible to get an infection from germs or skin trapped in the holes or reeds. And, as a rule, do not allow other people to play your harmonicas, just as you wouldn't let another person use your toothbrush.

Periodic cleaning is essential to maintaining a good sound as well. Dirt and tiny pieces of skin get trapped in the reeds and must be cleaned out before the reeds either buzz or stop sounding completely. Disassembly is simple and reveals a lot about how this instrument works. Just use a little screwdriver on the screws at the corners of the reed plates on the top and bottom of the harp. Then use rubbing alcohol to clean the reeds and comb with a Q-tip swab until the swab comes out clean.

Make sure not to lose the small screws and bolts that hold the harmonica together, as they are tough to replace. If you have access to a surgical clamp, it is a very useful tool that works great for holding and tightening the tiny parts. They can be purchased at any online surgical supply outlet.

New harmonicas generally don't require much cleaning, but always remember to clean old harmonicas before you play them. Dust and other unpleasant things may have settled inside the harp. Just run some warm water through the instrument (as long as it has a plastic comb) and then rap it several times with the holes facing down to get the excess water out.

Be careful not to bend or adjust the reed spaces, which are the spaces between the end of the reed and the hole in the reed plate, unless you are trying to change their sound characteristics. For example, to get overblows out of a difficult reed, it may be possible to bend the reed slightly toward the reed plate on draw notes and away from the reed plate on blow notes.

Attempting to tune the reeds on your own harmonica can make the harp unusable very quickly, but if you are inclined to try it, the way to do it is with a small, fine file like a jeweler's file, which can be found at jewelry supply houses online. To raise the pitch of a reed you would gently file the top of the reed near the tip, which will make the reed vibrate faster and thus raise the pitch of the note. To lower the pitch of a reed you would gently file the top of the reed near the base, which makes the reed vibrate more slowly and thus lowers the pitch of the note.

In case you need them, Lee Oskar makes replacement reed plates for their harmonicas and will also make special tunings for you upon request, but this gets pricey.

FACT

The original harmonicas only had half of the function of today's harmonicas. That's because they only had blow notes. Even though the concept of two-way reeds had been employed in instruments such as the accordion, it wasn't until a clever Hohner employee named Richter came along and applied it to the harmonica that each hole of the harp gained the ability to produce two notes.

If all of this sounds like a different language to you, don't worry. The next chapter will explain all the different parts of the harp.

Also, remember that to play the instrument one doesn't need an advanced knowledge of music theory, materials, science, or economic and historical trends in the harmonica industry. All you need is a relentless desire to play the harp. Playing the harmonica is supposed to be fun. The more you practice and fool around with it, the more tunes and tricks you'll add to your skill set. Carry it with you wherever you go, and play it whenever you have a chance. That is how every great harmonica player developed.

CHAPTER 2

The Basics

This chapter will take a look at the basic structure of the harmonica and the various parts that make it work, as well as how the notes are laid out on the instrument and some of the basic techniques that you'll need to play it. It will also examine how a major scale is played on the harmonica, and it will focus on some basic breathing techniques.

A Look Inside

The harmonica is made up of several different parts, as you can see from the exploded diagram in Figure 2-1.

FIGURE 2-1:
Exploded view
of the parts of
the harmonica

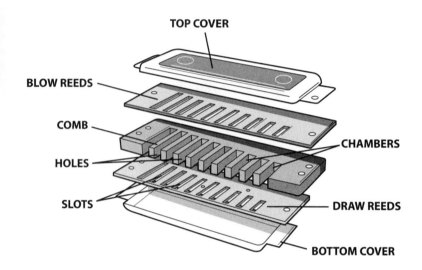

FIGURE 2-1: Exploded view of the parts of the harmonica

TOP COVER

BLOW REEDS

COMB

HOLES

SLOTS

CHAMBERS

DRAW REEDS

BOTTOM COVER

From top to bottom, there's the top cover; the top reed plate with the blow reeds; the comb, which has holes you blow or draw air through and chambers that direct the air to the reeds; the bottom reed plate with the draw reeds; and the bottom cover.

The Ten Holes

The diatonic harmonica has ten holes in the front of the comb, numbered 1 through 10 on the top reed plate, with 1 being the lowest-pitched notes and 10 being the highest notes. The comb itself is usually made of plastic or wood, although in some cases it could be made of metal. Behind the holes in the comb are the chambers, which direct air over the reeds. When you blow into a hole, the air passes through the chamber over the blow reed, causing it to vibrate, and out the slot. When you draw on a hole, the air enters through the slot and passes over the draw reed, causing it to vibrate, and exits out the chamber and hole.

Twenty Reeds

If you remove the top plate you'll see the top of the blow reed plate. Note that there are ten reeds welded to the plate under slots of the same length and width as the reed. You will also see on close inspection that the space between the reed and the slot is very small. This space is very specific, like the spacing on a spark plug, and as on a spark plug, this tiny space is where all of the excitement begins.

That's because the sound of the harmonica is created when the reed vibrates in its slot, creating sound waves in the air. The length of the reed and the speed at which it vibrates are what determine its pitch—the shorter the reed is, the faster it vibrates, and the higher the note it produces.

It is also the space between the reed and the slot that determines how hard and how precise your breath must be moving through the hole associated with that reed. You'll notice as the reeds become smaller on higher-pitched harmonicas that your breath control has to be more precise in order to get a clean and accurate tone. This means you'll have to get used to the specific demands of each key of the harmonica every time you start playing a new key, and experiment until you find the right feel for that harp.

QUESTION?

Why do harmonicas always stop working after a while?
Understanding how the harmonica deteriorates goes a long way toward understanding the nature and limitations of the instrument. Over time, as the reeds are played, the vibration creates microscopic fractures in the structure of the metal, similar to the way the wings of an airplane become fatigued after thousands of hours of bouncing through the sky. This is called "metal fatigue," and it can cause the reed to stick or even break.

If you then remove the bottom plate, you will see that there are ten more reeds welded to the plate on the side facing you. This tells you that these are the draw reeds, because the vibrating of the reed in the notched plate generates the sound, and the air is coming from above the reed. You will also notice that the lower reeds have a little more metal at the end farthest from the weld. This is to reduce the speed of the vibration, causing a lower-pitched note.

To sum up: You have two reed plates with ten reeds each, making twenty reeds that are played through the ten holes in the comb. Each reed is activated by either blowing air through a hole or drawing air through a hole, which passes through the space beneath the upper and lower exterior plates. That is how the harmonica is able to play its sweet music.

Blow Notes and Draw Notes

The diatonic harmonica has ten holes, and each hole has two reeds assigned to it. These reeds are activated by either blowing or drawing air through the holes in the harmonica. Therefore the instrument has ten blow notes and ten draw notes, giving it a basic range of nineteen notes (not twenty because the 2-hole draw and the 3-hole blow notes are exactly the same). Beyond this basic range many other notes can be produced on the harmonica using note-bending techniques. (More on these bending techniques in Chapter 5.)

The ten blow notes on the C diatonic harmonica, going from lowest pitch to highest, are C, E, G, C, E, G, C, E, G, C. The lowest C is the same note as middle C on a piano.

The ten draw notes on the C diatonic harmonica, going from lowest pitch to highest, are D, G, B, D, F, A, B, D, F, A.

FIGURE 2-2: Example of the ten blow notes

TRACK 2

FIGURE 2-3: Example of the ten draw notes

TRACK 3

The Three Octaves

The diatonic harmonica has a range of three octaves that are defined by the blow notes on holes 1, 4, 7, and 10. The range of an instrument is the number of notes that can be played on it, from the lowest note through the highest note the instrument can produce. An octave is defined by two notes with the same letter name that are 12 half steps apart, a half step being the smallest space between two notes in Western music. The higher octave note vibrates at twice the speed of the lower octave note, which is why the two notes sound the same. For example, the lowest C on the C diatonic harmonica, 1 blow, vibrates at 256 beats per minute (BPM) while the 4 blow C vibrates at 512 BPM.

FIGURE 2-4: Example of the three octaves of the harmonica

TAB: 1↑   4↑   7↑   10↑

TRACK 4

The Major Scale

The tuning of the diatonic harmonica is based on one major scale defined by the key the harmonica is in. In the case of the C diatonic harmonica, all the notes are based on the C-major scale. Although the blow notes on the C harp make up three C-major triads (the notes C, E, and G repeated three times with one more C on top), it's interesting to note that, because of the way the draw notes are laid out, each of the three octaves create different scales. Playing the notes consecutively beginning with hole 1 blow-draw, the first octave is C, D, E, G, G, B, C; the second octave is C, D, E, F, G, A, C; and the third octave is C, B, E, D, G, F, C, with A as the final draw note.

Holes 4 Through 7

Of the three different scales discussed above, the one place it's possible to play the full major scale in the key of the harp is between holes 4 and 7. This is achieved by playing the following pattern:

4 blow – 4 draw – 5 blow – 5 draw – 6 blow – 6 draw – 7 draw – 7 blow

If you're playing in the key of C and you want to play a major melody, such as "When the Saints Go Marching In," you would have to play it between holes 4 and 7.

Breathing Patterns

A very helpful hint when trying to play the harmonica well is to create a little tension in the airflow before you play a note. This can be accomplished by the way you breathe air through the harp or, more specifically, by keeping two "nonwords" or syllables in mind that you can use to determine your "attack" on a note—those syllable sounds are "Duh" and "Tuh."

The term *attack* refers to the way a note begins. A soft attack would be achieved by striking the note lightly, such as plucking a guitar string gently with the soft pad of your finger or hitting a piano key gently. A hard or sharp attack would be achieved by plucking a guitar string strongly with a pick or striking a piano key with force.

In the case of the harmonica a soft attack is achieved by blowing or drawing gently into the hole, starting with just enough air to make the reed begin to vibrate and then gently ramping up the amount of air to make the note sound fuller. To get a sharp attack on a harmonica blow note, you would build up some blow air pressure in your mouth and then release it suddenly into the hole by starting your release of air with a consonant sound like a "T." To get a sharp attack on a draw note, you would build up some draw air pressure in your mouth and then draw suddenly on the hole by starting your draw of air with a consonant sound like a "D."

To get a sharp attack on draw notes on the harmonica, when drawing air through the harp, put your tongue against the roof of your mouth as if to say "Duh" and then release the air flow making the reed vibrate cleanly and strongly from the very beginning of your note. You'll do the same thing to get a sharp attack on blow notes, except when blowing you'll use "Tuh" as your syllable. This will be discussed further in Chapter 6.

FACT

The earliest ancestor of the harmonica is the *sheng*, a 3,000-year-old Chinese instrument that earned the nickname "Chinese mouth organ" in the West. Air is blown or drawn through a mouthpiece connected to a base wind chamber, above which a series of bamboo pipes of various lengths are mounted. Each pipe has a free brass reed at the root, like a harmonica reed.

It is also important to note that you don't want to breathe through your nose while playing harmonica. Breathing through your nose while playing will make your sound weak and make it harder to get good, clean notes and bends. If you normally breathe through your nose, this will feel strange at first, but it will help your sound immensely.

The exception to this is an interesting technique called *circular breathing* that horn players as well as Yoga enthusiasts have probably heard of. Circular breathing allows a musician to play a continuous stream of notes indefinitely with no break for air between them. How is this possible? Here's the secret—the musician momentarily allows air pressure to build up in his mouth, cheeks, and throat, and for brief moments every now and then he uses that pressure to keep air flowing through the instrument while at the same time taking a quick breath through his nose, allowing the air to keep going. Some well-known harmonica players have used this technique, including Pat Missin and Howard Levy.

If you are aware and able to control your breathing in this circular way, you already have expert knowledge of breathing techniques, but if like most players you don't use this technique, you will have to learn to breathe in and out at alternating intervals and learn to develop a sense of when to inhale and exhale during your playing. One good place to start is to get used to breathing in or out as required at the end of each phrase you play, a *phrase* being a group of notes that expresses one musical idea. Eventually you won't even have to think about when to breathe because it will come naturally.

When practicing, you might hyperventilate and feel lightheaded. If you feel dizzy while you're practicing—stop playing immediately. Wait until you catch your breath and you feel normal before trying to play more. Over time, your stamina will improve and you'll be able to play for longer and longer periods of time.

Lastly on this topic, it might interest you to know that in some medical circles harmonica playing has been prescribed to help patients with breathing problems improve their breath control. So making beautiful music just may be good for your health!

Chords

In music theory, two notes played at the same time make an interval, and three or more notes played at the same time make a chord.

Major and minor chords are made up of intervals called *thirds*, which are formed when you play two notes of a scale that are separated by one note. For example, a C-major scale is made up of the notes C, D, E, F, G, A, B, C. If you play the notes C and E together, omitting the D in between, you have a third. Playing D and F together or E and G together also make thirds, and so on.

A *triad* is a three-note chord made of the first, third, and fifth notes of the scale. In the case of our C-major scale, the C-major triad is made of the notes C, E, and G. And you'll remember from above that the blow notes on the C diatonic harp are C, E, G, C, E, G, C, E, G, C.

So how convenient is that? Any three adjacent holes you blow together on the C diatonic harmonica form a C-major triad, each with different voicings.

The notes of chords can be played in different orders, and the order of notes in a chord is known as the chord's *voicing*. For example, the same C-major triad can be voiced, from lowest note to highest, either C-E-G, E-G-C, or G-C-E.

Playing three adjacent draw notes on the harmonica also creates triads. Playing holes 1-2-3 draw forms a G-major triad, as does playing 2-3-4 draw. Other triads formed by adjacent draw notes are:

- 3-4-5 draw = G7 sound (would be a full G7 with the 2 draw added)
- 4-5-6 draw = D minor
- 7-8-9 draw = G7 sound
- 8-9-10 draw = D minor

FIGURE 2-5: Example of a C-major chord

TAB: 1↑   2↑   3↑   (123)↑

TRACK 5

In the next chapter you'll learn about rhythm and the important part it plays in learning to play the harmonica.

CHAPTER 3

Understanding Rhythm

Rhythm is the pulse and the heartbeat of music. From the beginning of recorded history man has been playing drums and other percussion instruments. In ancient tribal dances the drums were what connected all the dancers together in a common rhythm. Drums perform the same function today in a modern rock, jazz, or blues band—all of the players sync up with the drummer and, by doing so, all of the players lock together into a common groove.

When to Play

When you're playing by yourself, you're free to experiment and go wherever your imagination takes you. You can start, stop, and veer down any path you like—and you should, because following your impulses and going wherever your curiosity leads you is an excellent way to learn about music.

But when you're playing with other people, or "playing ensemble," that all changes. Now your common objective with the other musicians becomes to sound as good as possible as a unit. This means you have to suppress your natural impulse to play constantly and start thinking about what's going to make the group sound best. Generally this means allowing the musical focus to be either on the group as a unit or on one musician at a time, with the other musicians "comping" for him—comping being a jazz term that means playing what sounds good with, or what complements the lead musician's solo.

Looking to interact with other harmonica players? Check out the many harmonica clubs that exist in practically every city. You can locate them by going to *www.Meetup.com* and typing in "harmonica" and your zip code. If there isn't a harmonica group already in place, you can list yourself as someone who's interested in having one.

Comping for another musician includes *not* playing anything that distracts from what the soloist is doing, but rather playing notes, chords, or phrases that enhance what the soloist is playing and spur him on to greater heights.

This section might as well be called "when *not* to play" because that's the real guiding factor in tasteful ensemble playing. Here are some of the basic rules:

- **Don't play when the singer is singing, except during breaks in the vocals.** A good way to practice this concept is to sing the song lyrics yourself and then fit harmonica phrases in the spaces between the vocal lines—this exercise automatically prevents you from playing over the vocals.

- **Don't play when someone else is taking a solo,** except for possibly comping as mentioned previously.
- **Don't play when the opening or closing melodies** are being stated (unless you're playing the exact melodies).
- **Don't play if you haven't figured out the sound of the chord progression yet,** or if you get confused about where you are in the progression during a song. Then jump in when you get your bearings.

Remember, when you're playing music with other musicians, choosing *not* to play sometimes and purposely leaving empty space for the other players to occupy can be just as musical as playing. And when it's your turn to play and solo you'll appreciate it when your fellow musicians support you in these ways.

Counting

Even when there is no drummer playing, every piece of music has its own rhythm and its own tempo, a musical word that describes the speed at which a piece is played. When an ensemble of musicians is playing without a drummer, all of the musicians know and are in agreement about what the rhythm and the tempo of the piece will be. In the same way, when you're playing a piece of music by yourself you'll need to have the rhythm and the tempo of the music in mind to play it with the right feel.

There are hundreds of annual harmonica festivals around the United States and around the world every year, where players and enthusiasts meet to revel in the instrument. These include the Spring Harmonica Festival in San Diego, California, the Buckeye Harmonica Festival in Columbus, Ohio, and the Atlantic Canada Harmonica Festival in Nova Scotia.

The beat of a song defines its rhythm and pace. It's the centerpiece of the music, around which everything else is built. The *beat* of a piece of music usually refers to the pulse of the note that gets one beat in the time signature that the piece is in—more on time signatures in the following section.

Before a band begins a song you'll often hear the bandleader or the drummer "count off" the time by saying "1-2-3-4" or something similar—this count is delivered at the exact speed the song will be played at, and this alerts all the other musicians about what pace they'll be playing and also what the length of one measure is.

Besides counting the beats of a measure, when you're first learning about chord progressions you might find yourself having to count the measures, or bars, themselves as they go by to keep track of where you are. A chord progression is the series of chords that are played to accompany the melody of a song. For example, a very common chord progression in blues is the 12-bar blues progression, also called a "12-bar blues." Just like it sounds, a 12-bar blues takes 12 measures to play through the entire chord progression one time. If you're trying to count measures in a progression, the way to do it is to replace the "1" of the 1-2-3-4 beat count in each measure with the measure number instead, which would look like this for a 12-bar blues:

One-2-3-4	Two-2-3-4	Three-2-3-4	Four-2-3-4
Five-2-3-4	Six-2-3-4	Seven-2-3-4	Eight-2-3-4
Nine-2-3-4	Ten-2-3-4	Eleven-2-3-4	Twelve-2-3-4

In the beginning, when you're just learning about rhythm and beats, you may find yourself spending a lot of time counting in your head—or even out loud—while you're playing to make sure you know where you are in the measure or in the chord progression. But as time goes by and you start to feel rhythm, beats, and progressions naturally you'll find that you don't have to count anymore because you'll know where you are by feel alone.

Time Signatures

The individual beats in a piece of music are divided into measures, also known as bars, which are repeating groups of beats. And a time signature is made up of two numbers that appear above and below each other, as in these examples:

$\frac{4}{4}$ or $\frac{3}{4}$, etc., which can also be represented as 4/4 and 3/4

These numbers appear in the first measure of a chart or score to tell you how to count the piece of music. The top number represents the number of beats in each measure, and the bottom number tells you what kind of note gets one beat. For example, in the second example above the "3" on top means there are three beats per measure, and the "4" on the bottom means that a quarter note gets one beat. Of these two numbers, the one that matters most in determining the feel of a piece of music is the top one—the number of beats per measure.

The most common time signature is 4/4. In this time there are four beats per measure, and the quarter note gets one beat. When the bandleader counts the song off with a "1-2-3-4" he is counting off one measure at the exact speed that you'll be playing the song.

There's virtually no limit to the number of possible time signatures. You can have as many beats as you want in a measure—a whole piece of music could be written as one measure if you wanted to go to extremes.

Each time signature has its own emotional feel. Besides 4/4 the most common time signatures and their feels are:

- 2/4 which has a hopping polka feel, counted 1-2, 1-2
- 3/4 which has a circular or waltz feel, counted 1-2-3, 1-2-3
- 5/4 which has a measure-of-three with a two-beat accent feel, counted 1-2-3-4-5, 1-2-3-4-5
- 7/4 which has a measure-of-four with a three-beat accent feel, counted 1-2-3-4-5-6-7, 1-2-3-4-5-6-7
- 11/4 which has a three-measures-of-three with a two-beat accent feel, counted 1-2-3-4-5-6-7-8-9-10-11, 1-2-3-4-5-6-7-8-9-10-11

But the fact is, you can create any time signature you want, assigning any number of beats to the measure and any note value as getting one beat.

Note Length Values

The lengths of notes are indicated through a system of note heads, note stems, and note flags. The head of the note is the oval that is either white or black in the center. The stem is the line that either rises or falls vertically from the note, and the flag is either a flag shape coming off of the end of the stem farthest from the note head, or a heavy horizontal line connecting two or more notes together. Here are examples of different kinds of notes and their values in 4/4 time:

- **Whole note =** oval note head with white center and no stem—gets four beats
- **Half note =** oval note head with a white center and a stem—gets two beats
- **Quarter note =** oval note head with a black center and a stem—gets one beat
- **Eighth note =** oval note head with a black center, a stem, and one flag—gets a half beat
- **Sixteenth note =** oval note head with a black center, a stem, and two flags—gets one quarter of a beat
- **Thirty-second note =** oval note head with a black center, a stem, and three flags—gets one eighth of a beat

Just so you understand the relationship between these different note values, one whole note is equal to two half notes, four quarter notes, eight eighth notes, sixteen sixteenth notes, or thirty-two thirty-second notes.

The National Harmonica League is a UK-based national harmonica club with many members in the United States. The fee to join is $30 per year for U.S. members, and the benefits include six issues of *Harmonica World* magazine per year, free ads in the magazine, and access to teachers and pro harp players. Go to *http://harmonica.co.uk* for more information and for the U.S. address to join.

FIGURE 3-1:
Types of notes

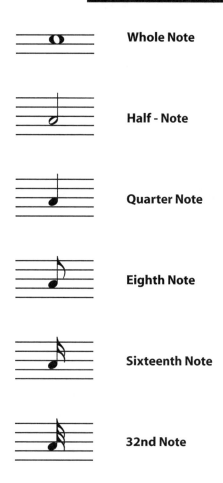

Whole Note

Half - Note

Quarter Note

Eighth Note

Sixteenth Note

32nd Note

Tap Your Foot

Tapping your foot connects your body physically to the rhythm of the piece of music you're playing or listening to. Best of all, this reaction to music is usually unconscious, so you can focus on the progression and on what you're playing without having to concentrate on this physical connection to the beat.

Some players say they have trouble tapping their foot to the beat, and that it just gives them another thing to think about while playing. The fact is that tapping your foot to the beat is a natural response to music that usually happens automatically—you shouldn't have to think about it to make it happen, the music should make it happen for you. If that's not happening for you yet, don't worry and don't try to force it. Once your time gets accurate and playing harmonica becomes more natural for you, you'll look down one day and find your foot tapping all by itself!

FACT

There are many harmonica-based ensembles, the most famous of which is the Harmonicats, an all-harmonica quartet that had a number one hit in 1947 with "Peg O' My Heart." Other famous harmonica groups include the Strnad Brothers, the Nostalgics, the Dave McKelvy Trio, and the Original Harmonica Band.

Metronome Usage

When most people start playing along with a metronome they become easily frustrated—what is wrong with this thing, and why does it keep speeding up or slowing down? Fact is, you have a natural tendency to speed up or slow down as you play, and the metronome—being a perfect timekeeper—lets you know every time you drift off the beat. That's what makes it the most valuable practice tool you'll want to throw out the window.

A metronome is simply a tool that establishes a steady, reliable beat. The classic metronome, invented in the early 1800s, is a mechanical device that winds up and has an arm that swings back and forth, with a counterweight attached to the arm to adjust the speed. Time in music is measured in beats per minute (BPM), and the arm of the metronome has notches with BPM speeds indicated where you move the counterweight to get the speed you desire. Mechanical metronomes also often have a bell or chime that can be set to ring on every second, third, fourth, fifth beat, etc., so you can practice playing in any time signature you want.

The latest metronomes are electronic devices that produce clicks at the exact BPM you dial in. Sometimes they have an image on a screen of the classic metronome arm swinging back and forth as a visual cue to accompany the click.

The metronome allows you to adjust the speed you're playing at to whatever pace is appropriate for the song or exercise you're working on. It's always best to begin a new exercise at a very slow speed and practice until you can play it perfectly—only then should you gradually speed the metronome up to play the exercise faster. Remember, slow and perfect beats fast and sloppy every time!

When you're playing with a metronome, try sometimes using it to represent just beats 2 and 4 instead of beats 1-2-3-4. Beats 2 and 4 are usually what's being played on the snare drum by the drummer when playing in 4/4 time, so it's good to get used to playing along with that feel. To do this you would set the metronome at half the speed you want to play at because the metronome is playing every other beat. Then each measure will sound like this: "1-click-3-click, 1-click-3-click."

FACT

The Guinness world record for the fastest harmonica player was established by Nicky Shane in California on September 8, 2005. The heavy-metal-style harmonica player astonished everyone by playing at the hair-on-fire speed of 285 beats per minute. You can hear Shane perform on his 2006 album *Heavy Metal Harmonica*.

Also, when you're practicing with a metronome it's a good idea to tap your foot along with the metronome clicks, which physically connects you to the beat, as previously stated. This will also get you used to tapping your foot to music and help make that second nature to you, as well as improving your internal sense of time.

The next chapter will look at the techniques for playing single notes, meaning one note at a time, on the harmonica.

CHAPTER 4

One Note at a Time

Now it's time to focus on some of the specific techniques you'll need to take command of the harmonica. These include learning to control your breath, shaping your mouth, and using your tongue in order to produce the notes and sounds you want on the instrument. In this chapter the focus will be specifically on the techniques you'll need to get clean single notes out of your harmonica.

4

Relax and Get Comfortable

The first thing you'll notice when picking up a harmonica is how easy it is to play chords and to pick out simple tunes right off the bat. This is one big reason why the harmonica has become such a popular instrument in folk music as well as in rock and jazz, and why hundreds of millions of them have been manufactured over the years.

Spending some time just breathing through your harmonica is a good way to get a sense of how the instrument feels and the degree to which you feel comfortable with it so far. In fact, most people get a sense of contentment just from hearing the sound the instrument makes when blown. It can be very relaxing just to breathe through the low end (holes 1-2-3) of the instrument and listen to the hypnotic alternating chords your breath produces as it blows and draws over the reeds. This is also a good focusing exercise to shift your mind from the other concerns of your day to preparing to play the harmonica.

If you then play around a little by just blowing and drawing chords up and down the instrument you'll begin to understand what your harmonica is capable of doing, and how your breath affects the low, middle, and high reeds differently. As you get up to the higher reeds and the space the air is coming through becomes smaller, the amount of air you can blow or draw through the reed is reduced, and thus you'll find it takes less air to move the reed and get the note. Consequently you'll be inhaling or exhaling less volume of air when playing at the higher end of the harp, and using more volume of air when playing at the lower end.

Breath Control

You'll notice as you play that you can only get a pleasant sound out of the reed when you're using just the right amount of breath. Use too much and it sounds forced, and the reed also may stick at times. Use too little and it sounds weak and breathy—not the sound you're going for. Throughout this book you will practice exercises and riffs that are going to teach you about breath control.

ALERT!

Spending extended periods of time practicing breath control can be difficult if you have trouble breathing from asthma or other respiratory problems, or even if you have no respiratory problems at all. Be careful not to overdo it! On the plus side, harmonica playing has been shown to be an effective therapy for respiratory ailments, to the point where many hospitals now offer special harmonica classes.

Singers use a technique called *diaphragmatic breathing*. The diaphragm is a band of muscle just below your lungs. Try breathing deeply, putting your hand on your stomach and, using only your breath, see if you can make your hand move outward with your stomach. Feel it as you do, then expel the air slowly and deliberately until you feel you cannot exhale any more. Do this exercise three times in a row. When you're doing it correctly you will feel noticeably full of air, and if you practice this regularly you'll have more breath to control as well as better ability to control it. Many experienced players do this every time before they begin to practice just to wake up their lungs.

You might find as you're playing that you either run completely out of air, or your lungs become full from playing draw notes. This happens to everybody, but if you're aware of the problem, you can easily learn to avoid it. The way to do that is to take or expel little breaths right on the beat. Any of the beats of the measure will do for this, although you might find that the 1 or the 4 beats are best because they're naturally at the end of many phrases. The important thing is to do this between the phrases or ideas that you're playing, as opposed to interrupting a phrase to take or expel a breath.

ESSENTIAL

When playing draw notes on the low end of the harmonica you might find the sound you're producing to be weak, muffled, or lower than the correct pitch. This is the result of choking the reeds by forcing too much air through them. To avoid this, reduce the amount of air you're using on the problem notes, and try adjusting your mouth and throat positions.

Most people breathe through their nose and mouth or just through their nose. Harmonica playing is an exercise in breath control, and if you are breathing through your nose you are not putting all of your breath into the art of playing. Learning how not to breathe through your nose while playing requires that you think about it while you play, at least until it becomes second nature. This is true for the diaphragmatic breathing as well.

How to Hold Your Harmonica

Finding the most comfortable position for you to hold your harmonica is essential to developing your own style of play. That said, there are some basic rules that apply:

- Don't block the comb with your fingers—you don't want your hands to impede airflow through the instrument.
- Begin by holding it on one or both sides with your thumb and forefinger. This is helpful at first because you want to see which holes you are playing when practicing techniques to get single notes.
- The standard way to hold the harmonica is to place the left side of the harp into the crook between your thumb and forefinger in a comfortable but firm way, allowing your thumb to hold up the base of the harp and your finger to run along the top. You want to still be able to see the hole numbers on the top plate going from 1 to 10 from left to right.
- Be sure to leave space for your lips on the two outer plates.

FIGURE 4-1:
Holding the
harmonica

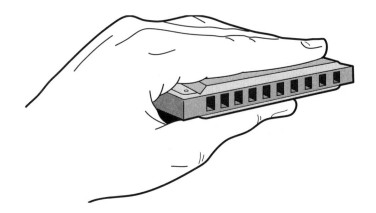

Notice that your three remaining fingers are sort of just hanging out and don't seem to be doing anything except maybe getting in the way. Hold your fingers together and make sort of a flat surface jutting out from the top of the harmonica. Then you can take your other hand and create a cavity in your two hands through which air can flow but which will mute the sound as it comes through the harp.

FACT

The smallest harmonica manufactured is the Hohner Little Lady, which is 1⅜ inches long and has four holes with eight reeds. The largest is the Hohner 48 Chord harmonica, two harps mounted above and below each other, which measures a whopping 23" long and has 96 double holes with 384 reeds.

With a little practice you can then open and close that gap while you play, creating a vibrato similar to what a trumpet player does with a mute getting that "*wa-wa*" sort of effect. This cavity you have created between your hands is where you will want to put a microphone. (Microphone techniques are discussed in Chapter 12.)

Techniques for Playing Single Notes

There are three commonly used techniques for playing single notes on a harmonica: lip blocking, lip pursing, and tongue blocking. The first is a simplified method that's easy for beginners to grasp quickly. The second calls for you to use the muscles on the sides of your mouth to direct air through specific holes on the harp. The third is pretty much what the name sounds like—using your tongue to block some of the holes, which your mouth encompasses to narrow your breath down to a single note. All three methods are useful when playing and should be learned in order to have the broadest range of available sounds in your skill set.

Lip-Blocking Method

Lip blocking is the most simplified method of achieving single notes on the harmonica. That's because the simple act of tilting the back of the harmonica up as you play has the effect of positioning the lips in a way that allows your breath to be directed into only one hole at a time. Try it. Position your lips so that you're blowing into three holes like you're playing a triad, and then tilt the back of the harmonica up until your lower lip naturally closes and blocks the holes on the sides, allowing just the center hole note to sound clearly. It happens automatically!

Pursed-Lip Method

Lip pursing is the method by which air is directed through the harp using the muscles on both sides of your mouth. This is best achieved by puckering your mouth as if you were going to kiss someone while leaving some space in the middle for air to move through. You might get the image of a goldfish when you look at yourself in the mirror doing this without the harp. Your tongue is used to help direct the air as well.

The back part of your tongue is pulled back as if to touch the roof of your mouth, but not quite touching it. The tongue comes down in an S-curve shape that creates a directed flow of air which, combined with your pursed lips, sends the flow of air directly through the hole. Moving your tongue back and forth will help in other ways, too, which will be described in Chapter 5. Practice this until you can get clean single notes all the way up and down the harmonica, drawing and blowing.

FIGURE 4-2:
Mouth in pursed
position

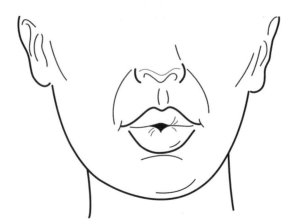

Tongue-Blocking Method

Tongue blocking is achieved by placing your mouth so that it covers four holes. Then, using your tongue, block the three holes to the right or left, allowing air to only reach the fourth hole on either side of your mouth. This should produce a clean sound blowing or drawing. Practice this until you can do it on either side of your mouth, depending on which note you are trying to get.

FIGURE 4-3:
Tongue-block-
ing position of
lips and tongue

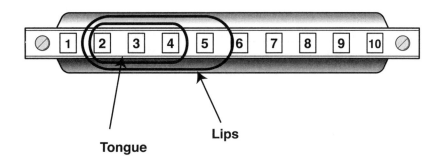

Lips

Tongue

Exercises for Playing Single Notes

Here are some exercises for playing single notes on the harmonica. Achieving clean single notes on the harmonica is one of the most important parts of being able to play well. The first method that most people learn is how to play a single note by tongue blocking. You'll hear an example of this on Track 6. Notice that only a single note was being played—no other reeds were vibrating at the same time as the one note.

FIGURE 4-4: Single note with tongue blocking

TRACK 6

TAB: 4↓

Pursed-Lip Method

Embouchure is a musical term for how your mouth is used to work an instrument. All wind instruments, which are played by a person forcing air thru them with his or her mouth, must have an embouchure. Saxophones, flutes, trumpets, and harmonicas are all instruments with different embouchures.

In the case of the harmonica you create the single note embouchure by pursing the sides of your mouth, leaving the upper and lower lips loose as if you were going to kiss someone, as stated above. You then place your mouth against the harmonica, allowing your upper lip to seal to the top of the harmonica and your lower lip to seal to the bottom. At this point you should be able to tighten the sides of your mouth to direct the air through a single hole. It may take a considerable amount of practice before you're able to get a single note clean using this method, but it is worth it!

It is important to keep the upper and lower parts of your lips loose and not press too hard against the upper and lower plates on the harp, but only press hard enough to create a seal against air escaping. The sides of the mouth are tensed to allow for directing air. Keeping your lips moist is also essential for creating a good seal to the harp and for allowing movement along its surface. You might be tempted to try using oil or some other lubricant to reduce the friction of your lips on the instrument, or to create a better seal. However, you should avoid using oils to achieve this. Licking is sufficient for playing the harmonica.

FACT

President Abraham Lincoln reportedly played the harmonica, and it was noted by historians that he carried one around in his pocket with him. He even took the time while he was president to write a letter to the head of the Hohner Harmonica Company expressing the joy he got from playing his Hohner harmonica.

Here's a simple exercise you can do to try to get clean notes using this method. On Track 7 you'll hear each hole on the C diatonic harmonica blown and then drawn individually. Try getting each note to sound as clean as possible before moving to the next note. Don't be discouraged if you have trouble getting clean single notes at first. With practice you'll be able to get nice, clean single notes out of every reed in your harmonica.

FIGURE 4-5: Pursed-lip exercise—to get clean single notes

TAB: 1↑ 1↓ 2↑ 2↓ 3↑ 3↓ 4↑ 4↓ 5↑ 5↓ 6↑ 6↓ 7↑ 7↓ 8↑ 8↓ 9↑ 9↓ 10↑10↓

TRACK 7

Chapter 5 will get deep into the techniques you'll need to bend notes on your harmonica.

Bending Notes

Now that you've learned to play single notes on the harmonica cleanly here's something a little more advanced—bends. Bending notes is one of the most important techniques in harmonica playing. Not only is it a great tool for expressing emotion in your music, it also adds several notes to the scale that the harmonica is capable of playing. Bending is an elusive technique that takes time to master, but once you learn the skill, it will add tremendously to your range as a player.

Bent and Blue Notes on Your Harmonica

As previously discussed, there are a lot of notes in the chromatic scale that are not part of the structure of the diatonic harmonica and cannot be played as normal blow or draw notes. However, it is possible to get some of these notes by using the technique called bending.

Bending a note means changing the pitch of the note, shifting the pitch either higher or lower than the original note being played. Notes are generally bent either a half step or a whole step up or down from the original note, although on some instruments they can be bent considerably further. On the harmonica, the largest possible bend is one and a half steps down, played on the 3-hole draw.

Bending can be done with both the draw notes and the blow notes on a harmonica and will achieve notes in between the notes built into the harp. Many of these "in-between" notes are referred to as *blue notes*, which are the notes that give the blues its classic sound.

Blue notes are changes made to the major scale, specifically a *flatted third* and a *flatted seventh* note, that create harmonic tension between sounds usually identified with a major scale and a minor scale, resulting in the classic blues sound mentioned above. A *flatted fifth* is also frequently used as an additional blue note.

A *flatted note* means a note that's lowered one half step, and the terms *third*, *fifth*, and *seventh* refer to the position of the notes in the scale. In the case of the C-major scale, which the C diatonic harmonica is based on, the notes of the scale are C, D, **E**, F, **G**, A, **B**, C. As you can see, the third note of the scale is the E, the fifth note is the G, and the seventh note is the B. Therefore the flatted third would be created by lowering the E one half step to E♭, the flatted fifth by lowering the G to G♭, and the flatted seventh by lowering the B to B♭.

The most prominent *blues scale* that's used to play over blues chord progressions employs all three of these flatted blue notes in this manner: C, **E♭**, F, **F♯**, G, **B♭**, C. Besides having the flatted third and the flatted seventh, this scale also uses both the flatted fifth (shown in the example as F♯, which is the same note as G♭) and the normal fifth, G, as consecutive notes.

FACT

The earliest blues recordings were made using wax cylinders. Thomas Edison himself, who was responsible for inventing very early recording equipment, was also responsible for making many of these recordings in the early 1920s, documenting artists including The Original Memphis Five, The Georgia Melodians, Elsie Clark, and Clarence Williams & Eva Taylor.

Bent notes on the harmonica are achieved by directing the force of the air through the hole in such a way that it actually creates vibration in both the draw and the blow reed at the same time. By using this method you can create tones that occur in between the normal tones of the harmonica. These bent notes or blue notes are essential to playing "cross harp," or blues harmonica. Track 8 contains an example of blues harmonica.

FIGURE 5-1: Blues harp example

TRACK 8

Draw Bends

Most of the time when you are listening to great blues harmonica, you are hearing the artist playing primarily draw notes, and many of those are bent draw notes. This is what is called playing cross harp, or playing in second position.

A *draw bend* is achieved by directing the air you draw through a hole so that it pulls both the draw reed and the blow reed simultaneously, creating a new note that is neither of the reeds' natural tunings. The overall effect of a draw bend is always to pull the pitch of the note down.

On the C diatonic harmonica the 2 hole can be bent as far as a whole step below its natural note, moving from a G down to an F. You can also get the F♯, or half-step bend, by manipulating the airflow. That's three clean notes from a single draw hole. This is not easy to achieve and will require many hours to perfect, so don't give up. Being able to draw bend makes the difference between sounding like Dusty out on the range or like your favorite blues harmonica player. Draw bends expand the range of the instrument tenfold.

FACT

The Hohner XB-40 Extreme Bending harmonica has note-bending capacity never seen on previous instruments. While normal diatonic harps can only be bent a half step or more on eight of the nineteen notes, the XB-40 allows every note on the instrument to be bent a whole step using normal bending technique, thanks to twenty extra reeds.

When you're trying to get a bend, please remember that it takes experimentation until you find the right "mouth" for it. Try going through these steps:

1. Using your correct embouchure for a single note, draw the 2 hole on your harmonica. Listen to its pure sound, nice and clean and clear, before you attempt to get your bend.
2. Take a moment to be aware of where in your mouth you have placed your tongue and how much air you are drawing to get that nice, clean unbent sound.
3. Using the same amount of air pressure on the draw, try pulling the back of your tongue toward the back of your throat. This causes the air, even though it's drawn at roughly the same pressure, to move through a more constricted passageway and thus to enter the hole at a higher rate of speed, which will create more pressure on the reed and produce a change in the note. Usually these first bends you try sound awful and are nearly impossible to maintain, so don't get discouraged.
4. As you're practicing, be aware of your breath and how it changes as it is being redirected through your mouth. Changing the tongue's position will make it possible to find and learn just the right point and airflow you need to create the bend.
5. Practice this until you can get a full step bend to the F note on this hole.

Eventually you will be able to get the full bend and the half-step bend and, if you are very good, all of the semitones in between.

It is possible to get draw bends from different holes, and you should experiment with all of the holes to see what you can get. Every draw reed gets its bend from the same method, so once you have found it you won't forget it; you will only need to adjust it slightly for each reed that you can bend. The hardest part once you have the basic approach is to not be satisfied until you can get the bend notes clean and clear.

Here is an example of a draw bend. The 2-hole draw is played to create the bent note. Both of those tones are coming from the single 2 hole.

FIGURE 5-2: Draw bend

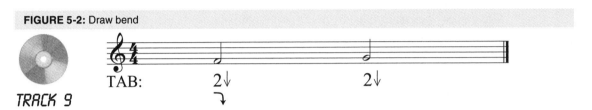

TRACK 9

A simple exercise you can try to get your bends in really good shape is to just practice them over and over again, seeing if you can find each individual tone that you can get with your bend. Now here's the exercise: The player on Track 10 is going to play the 2 draw, then the 3 draw, and the 4 draw, bending each note as he goes up the scale. You should try bending all the notes on your harmonica. You'll find that you can get many tones in between if you practice enough.

FIGURE 5-3: Draw bend exercise

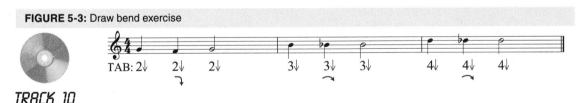

TRACK 10

Blow Bends and Overblows

Blow bends are similar to draw bends, only they're a lot more difficult to play. The basic idea is the same as the draw bend, but it is executed using the blow rather than the draw. The approach is similar as well. It requires a lot of experimentation and then practice once you have found the right mouth and tongue positions. Blow bends also lead to overblows.

An overblow is yet another additional note that can be gotten out of your harmonica. Overblows work differently than blow bends. A blow bend vibrates both reeds simultaneously to produce the bend effect, while an overblow jams one of the reeds while vibrating the other reed to create an overtone.

Friction between your mouth and the harmonica will interfere with your technique. Be sure your lips are moist at all times when you're playing, and lick the parts of the harp your mouth will be touching, both before you play and periodically while you're playing for maximum mobility.

While draw bends and blow bends can only lower the pitch of a note, overblows have the effect of raising the note—in some cases as much as a minor third up—by sounding an overtone of the reed pitch instead of the reed pitch itself. And once you get the overblow overtone to sound, it's further possible to bend that note slightly lower.

An *overtone* is another note created by the vibration caused by playing your original note. Every note has several overtones above it. You can hear an example of how overtones occur by doing this exercise: while singing one constant note, move your mouth very slowly from a tight "ooooooooh" sound to a wide open "aaaaaaaah" sound. As your mouth opens, you will hear the natural overtones of the note you're singing come in one at a time above the original pitch. It's wild!

Overblows are an advanced technique that is hard to master and that also requires that your harmonica be set up in a special way with the reeds very close to the reed plate. So don't be discouraged if you can't play one early in your harmonica career.

Here is what a blow bend sounds like.

FIGURE 5-4: Blow bend

TAB: 7↑

Classic Riffs with Draw Bends

Once you have achieved a certain amount of control over your bends and have gotten as many of them as you can find out of your C harmonica, you will want to use these new tools to create "riffs." A riff is a series of notes that create a musical idea or phrase. Riffs are often used as the building blocks or primary musical ideas of a song.

One classic riff that most people would recognize is the "Mannish Boy" or "Bad to the Bone" riff. This is a great example of how a musical idea or phrase is used to create a whole song. In fact, this riff is so complete that a harmonica alone is enough to play the song.

The first of our classic blues riffs is one of the most common you'll hear in blues. It's famously played in the classic, "Mannish Boy," by McKinley Morganfield, better known as Muddy Waters.

FIGURE 5-5: Classic riff with draw bend 1

TRACK 12

This riff is played by using:

1 draw - 2 draw bend - 1 draw - 2 draw bend - 2 draw unbent

This riff is often used in blues to punctuate the space that occurs between the singing of the vocal parts of a song. Typically the vocals and the harp riff would alternate in this way: counting each 4/4 measure as "1-and-2-and-3-and-4-and," the vocal line would be sung over counts "and-2-and-3" while the harmonica riff would be played over counts "and-4-and-1." So the overall effect would sound like this:

"Gypsy woman told my mother" (play riff) "Before I was born" (play riff), and so on.

Here are some other classic blues riffs that feature draw bends:

FIGURE 5-6: Classic riff with draw bend 2

TRACK 13

Here is another classic riff for you to try at home.

FIGURE 5-7: Classic riff with draw bend 3

TRACK 14

Here is the classic Fannie Mae riff.

FIGURE 5-8: Classic riff with draw bend 4

TRACK 15

The final example is a little bit more advanced: it combines a trill, draw bends, and rhythm exercise all combined into one.

With an arsenal that includes clean single notes and draw bends alone you should be able to play many of the great tried and true harmonica riffs.

FIGURE 5-9: Classic riff with draw bend 5

TRACK 16

TAB: 2↓   2↓   1↓   2↓   3↓   4↑

TAB: (45)↓〜〜〜〜〜〜〜〜〜〜   4↑   3↓   2↓   1↓

TAB: 2↓   2↓   1↓   2↓   3↓   4↑

TAB: (45)↓〜〜〜〜〜〜〜〜〜〜   4↑   3↓   1↓

TAB: 2↓   2↓   1↓   2↓   3↓   4↑

TAB: (45)↓〜〜〜〜〜〜〜〜〜〜   4↑   3↓   2↓   2↑

TAB: 2↓   2↓   1↓   2↓   3↓   4↑   4↓   4↓   4↓ 3↓ 2↓   2↓

Trills

A trill is defined as two notes played in rapidly alternating manner. On the harmonica a trill is created either by using your mouth to move between two holes, or by moving the harmonica itself across two holes to create a continuous sound that plays two notes one after the other. Both methods of achieving this trill effect are valid and may be used. The idea is to get the notes to sound clearly and in the right rhythm.

Trills are one of the more dynamic riffs in harmonica playing. A trill can be clean or bent as the player wishes, and you know you're doing it well when it sounds clear and not too "breathy." For instance, in the next track the player will play a trill on the 4-5 draw. Notice that bending the notes while playing the trill works very effectively and creates a nice dynamic.

FIGURE 5-10: Trills

TAB: (45)↓   (45)↓   (45)↓   (45)↓

TRACK 17

Slurs

A slur is defined as a group of notes played together smoothly with one note flowing directly into the next, as opposed to articulating each note individually. On the harmonica slurs are often created when, instead of playing only the single notes that are part of the melody of the song, a player plays all of the notes in between on the harp by passing over them quickly. It is an effective technique for adding tension to the song by creating a quick buildup to the next note. What is important about playing a slur is that it sounds deliberate and that you don't spend too much time on one of the in-between notes. Otherwise it will sound sloppy, as though the player isn't in control of the instrument. This technique can be effective when soloing to add tension or to bring your solo to a resolution, as in the following example.

FIGURE 5-11: Slurs

TAB: 5↓ 4↓ 3↓ 2↓

Riff Example

4↓ 5↓ 4↓ 3↓ 2↓

TRACK 18

Exercises for Playing Bends

Here's the most important thing to remember when trying to get your bends right—if they are not clear and in control, then you haven't got it yet. Each note needs to sound correct, meaning that it's bent to exactly the right degree, and to accomplish this your breath needs to be right on target. Try to get every bend you can out of your harmonicas and develop them as you continue to learn and practice.

FACT

The Bendometer Playing System is an interesting piece of shareware that uses a software program and a microphone connected to your computer to teach you how to play accurate bends. The program works like a tuner and shows you the notes you're playing on the computer screen. Find it at *http://harpsoft.com/subscribe/subscribe.html*.

Try each bend going from the 1 hole to the 10 hole, and once you get one you can keep trying to get the others. Your patience and practice will eventually reward you with a much bigger musical vocabulary. The harmonica is an easy instrument to play, but it takes a lifetime to master. Practice the exercises on Tracks 19 and 20 until they become second nature to you.

Exercise 1 for Playing Bent Notes

In this exercise we'll be hitting half-step bends on holes 1, 3, 4, and 5.

FIGURE 5-12: Exercise for playing bends 1

TRACK 19

Exercise 2 for Playing Bent Notes

It is extremely important that you get the 2-draw bend—it is a whole-step bend, and it must be clean every single time for you to get the resolution of your cross-harp songs.

FIGURE 5-13: Exercise for playing bends 2

TRACK 20

Next, Chapter 6 will look at the rhythmic accompaniment that supports harmonica playing, and how to interact with it.

CHAPTER 6

Rhythm Accompaniment

You've already learned how to use your tongue to get single notes on the harmonica. But the tongue is capable of much more than that. It can also be used to create alternating chords and octaves, to create syncopated rhythms, and to alternate between single notes and chords. In this chapter you will learn the techniques you'll need to create rhythmic parts on the harp, as well as get a taste of what it's like to play with another rhythm instrument.

Advanced Tongue Techniques

Tongue techniques add depth and variety to your play, and effective use of advanced tongue techniques can signal the difference between being a good harp player and being a great one. Basically tongue technique is just what it sounds like—using your tongue to block specific holes while allowing only the holes you want to get air. It may sound simple, but getting it to work well can be a little daunting.

Try using the tongue-blocking method you already know to get a single note. Position your mouth as if to play a four-note chord using holes 1-2-3-4 blow. Then use your tongue to block holes 1 through 3, and allow the air to move past your tongue and play just the 4 hole. This will sound a single note. Try doing this exercise all the way up the harmonica. Then try blocking the other side, covering the three upper holes and allowing the lowest note in the group to sound. This technique will work for both blow and draw notes.

Playing Octaves

This same tongue-blocking concept can be modified to get octaves as well. Octaves are often used to add strength to a given note by doubling it. In music the word *doubling* means using two voices to play the same note, phrase, or part.

FACT

If you're the type who thinks that every phone call could benefit from a harmonica intro, then harmonica ringtones are for you. They come in all styles from short phrases to full four-measure lines. One user-friendly site where you can find them is *www.audiosparx.com*. Look under "woodwinds" to find the harmonica ringtones.

Octaves are achieved on the harmonica by modifying the tongue-blocking technique used to play single notes. In this case the tongue is used to block the middle holes between the octave notes you're trying to play, allowing the air to pass on both sides of your tongue until you have two clean octave notes sounding on the harmonica simultaneously. Try it now by positioning your mouth as if to play the same four-note chord using holes 1-2-3-4 blow that you used above for tongue blocking—but instead of blocking all but one hole, use your tongue to block holes 2 and 3, allowing your air to flow into holes 1 and 4. When done properly you should hear two clean C notes that are an octave apart.

Among the blow notes the octaves that are available to you occur between holes 1 and 4 (C), 2 and 5 (E), 3 and 6 (G), 4 and 7 (C), 5 and 8 (E), 6 and 9 (G), and 7 and 10 (C).

Among the draw notes the available octaves occur between holes 1 and 4 (D), 3 and 7 (B), 4 and 8 (D), 5 and 9 (F), and 6 and 10 (A). Note that the last four of these octaves require you to block three holes with your tongue, which is difficult even for experienced harp players, so they are shown more for your reference than as a suggested exercise.

Practice this octave technique until you can get a clean octave sound between the combinations of holes listed above. This technique is a building block for learning the other advanced tongue-blocking techniques to follow.

Tongue Slapping

Tongue slapping is a technique that employs basic tongue blocking and adds the action of moving the tongue on and off of the comb to block and unblock holes in order to change the number of notes being played at one time.

You can try tongue slapping by playing one of your octaves and then moving your tongue off and on the middle holes that it's blocking. Notice that the sound shifts back and forth from the octave sound to the full chord sound.

Tongue Vamping

Tongue vamping combines the techniques of tongue blocking and tongue slapping to create a repeating rhythmic pattern of alternating single note and chord sounds.

The idea of tongue vamping is to use a phrase or idea repetitively within the rhythm of a song, which has the effect of creating the sound of a single note melody being accompanied by chords, all being played on one harmonica.

Here's an example of tongue vamping. This concept combines two techniques: playing an octave in your harmonica by blocking holes 2 and 3 while playing holes 1 and 4. First you'll hear all four holes, and then you'll hear holes 2 and 3 blocked so that you can hear the octave. By rhythmically lifting and replacing the tongue over holes 2 and 3 you create the vamp, and it sounds like this.

FIGURE 6-1: Tongue vamping

TRACK 21

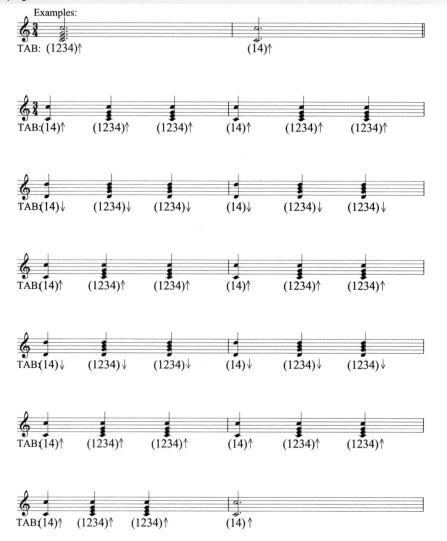

Tongue Shuffle

In the examples of 4/4 time up to this point the measures have been divided either into their individual four beats or into an "eighth-note feel," where each count of the measure gets two beats (counted "1-and-2-and-3-and-4-and").

A *shuffle* rhythm uses a different way of approaching 4/4 time. In this case each of the four beats in the measure is divided into three equal parts known as *triplets*. Each measure would be counted "1-and-a-2-and-a-3-and-a-4-and-a." The rhythm is then further refined by accenting just the first and last beat of each group of triplets, which looks like this:

1-and-**a-2**-and-**a-3**-and-**a-4**-and-**a 1**-and-**a-2**-and-**a-3**-and-**a-4**-and-**a**

To *accent* means to play a beat or note more loudly than the beats or notes surrounding it, thereby emphasizing it. The overall effect is to create a kind of skipping rhythm that's quite driving and full of forward motion. In fact, some people like to say that it's easy to remember what a shuffle rhythm sounds like because it sounds just like its name: "shuffle-shuffle-shuffle-shuffle."

On harmonica, a *tongue shuffle* combines the techniques of tongue vamping, tongue slapping, octaves, and single notes to create a shuffle rhythm.

FACT

Some great examples of the shuffle rhythm can be heard on songs such as "Key to the Highway," the Broonzy/Segar song played often by Eric Clapton; "On the Road Again," by Canned Heat; and "Sweet Home Chicago," the Robert Johnson song played by Muddy Waters, Buddy Guy, Clapton, and practically every other blues artist.

Here's a cool shuffle phrase you can try. It uses the shuffle rhythm described above, but the phrase begins on the last triplet note of the previous measure, so the count will shift to look like this:

a-1-and-**a-2**-and-**a-3**-and-**a-4**-and

Then play each of the accented beats as follows:

a-1	draw 2
a	1-2-3-4 draw
2	1-2-3-4 blow
a	1-2-3-4 blow
3	1-2-3-4 draw
a	1-2-3-4 draw
4	2 blow

An example of the shuffle rhythm can be heard on Track 25.

Articulation Syllables

When someone is speaking or singing, if they are sloppy or unintelligible it distracts from what they are trying to say. Harmonicas, like all musical instruments, are vessels used to express the feelings and ideas of the player. A great player is one who masters the ability to express those feelings and thoughts clearly through his instrument, without obvious technical errors, and a big step toward that goal is being able to play notes cleanly.

Creating rhythms also requires an ability to control the attack on the harp, so at this point it becomes more important for you to have a good understanding of how to create a sharp attack on your notes using articulation syllables. *Articulation syllables* are letter sounds like "D" and "T" that you make with your mouth at the beginning of each note to release a concentrated amount of air that produces the hard attack. Using these non-words like "duh" and "tah" to create better sounding notes will allow you to play more cleanly and is most important to playing well.

The word *attack* is used in music to describe how a note starts. It can start smoothly using just breath, or it can start suddenly. Articulation syllables are letter sounds used to create a sudden attack. The "T" sound is used for sudden blow notes. The "D" sound is used for sudden draw notes.

FIGURE 6-2: Articulation syllables

TRACK 22

Simple Rhythms and Syncopated Rhythms

The word syncopated means the emphasizing of beats that are normally not the strong or accented beats in the rhythm you're playing. This is accomplished by accenting these weak beats.

For example, in 4/4 time where each measure has four beats, a simple rhythm would emphasize the first beat in each measure, like this:

1-2-3-4 **1**-2-3-4 **1**-2-3-4 **1**-2-3-4

Or it might emphasize all four beats equally. By contrast, a syncopated rhythm might accent the second and fourth beat of each measure, as is common in rock, blues, and country music, like this:

1-**2**-3-**4** 1-**2**-3-**4** 1-**2**-3-**4** 1-**2**-3-**4**

Another way to create syncopation is to add accents that fall between the beats of the measures, such as by accenting the first and fourth beats of each measure and then adding another accent on the half-beat (also known as the "and of the beat" because of the way it's counted) between the fourth and first beats, like this:

1-and-2-and-3-and-**4**-**and** **1**-and-2-and-3-and-**4**-**and**

Syncopated rhythms add tension and energy to music, making it sound spicier and more exotic when that is what's called for. You normally wouldn't want to add syncopation to a song with a simple rhythm such as

"Twinkle, Twinkle Little Star," a song that emphasizes all four beats of the measure equally, but if you were to experiment by adding the syncopated beat above with the 4-and-1 accents you would find that the syncopated beat adds energy and drive to the song that wasn't there before, and makes the song sound very different.

When you're practicing it's tempting to play all the things you can already play well, but if you want to expand your technique it's important to purposely take yourself out of your "comfort zone" by trying things you don't know how to play or aren't already good at. Overcoming these challenges will increase your confidence and your abilities.

The following examples illustrate the difference between simple rhythms and syncopated rhythms. The first example is a simple rhythm and the second is a syncopated rhythm.

FIGURE 6-3A: Simple rhythms

TRACK 23

TAB: 1↓ 2↑ 3↑ 4↑   4↓ 4↑ 3↓ 2↓   1↓ 2↑ 3↑ 4↑   4↓ 4↑ 3↓ 2↓

TAB: 1↓ 2↑ 3↑ 4↑   4↓ 4↑ 3↓ 2↓   1↓ 2↑ 3↑ 4↑   4↓ 4↑ 3↓ 2↓

FIGURE 6-3B: Syncopated rhythms

TRACK 23

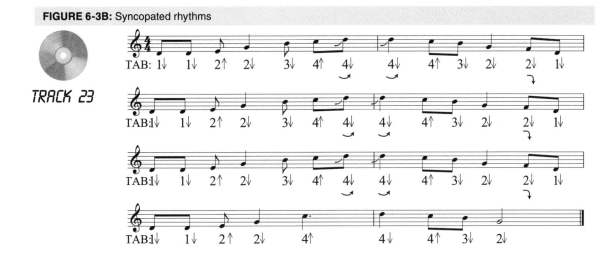

Rhythmic Exercises

In the following rhythmic exercises you'll have the opportunity to combine many of the techniques you've learned up to this point—including playing single notes and chords, using syncopation, and playing rhythm—into cohesive musical phrases.

Practice these exercises often and the techniques will mesh and support each other, becoming new tools you can command.

ALERT!

When traveling with your harmonicas remember that they can be a cause for concern at airport security. It's best if you announce that you have harmonicas before you put your bag through the X-ray machine—but don't be surprised if they ask you to play something to make sure you're not just using those harps for bomb parts!

Here's a rhythm exercise for you to try. This one involves going from chords to single notes and back to chords. You'll hear it start slowly, and then it will speed up.

FIGURE 6-4: Rhythm exercise 1

TRACK 24

TAB: 2 ↓   (1234)↓   (1234)↑   (1234)↑   (1234)↓   (1234)↓   (1234)↑   2↓

TAB: (1234)↓   (1234)↑   (1234)↑   (1234)↓   (1234)↓   (1234)↑   2↓

TAB: (1234)↓   (1234)↑   (1234)↑   (1234)↓   (1234)↓   (1234)↑   2↓

TAB: (1234)↓   (1234)↑   (1234)↑   (1234)↓   (1234)↓   (1234)↑   2↓

TAB: (1234)↓   (1234)↑   (1234)↑   (1234)↓   (1234)↓   (1234)↑   2↓

TAB: (1234)↓   (1234)↑   (1234)↑   (1234)↓   (1234)↓   (1234)↑

TAB: (345) ↓

Here's an example of how the harmonica interacts with another instrument playing a rhythmic feel. Try learning the harmonica riff demonstrated on Track 25, and then try playing it along with the recorded track to get the feel of playing with a guitar player.

FIGURE 6-5A: Rhythm exercise 1—Blues shuffle

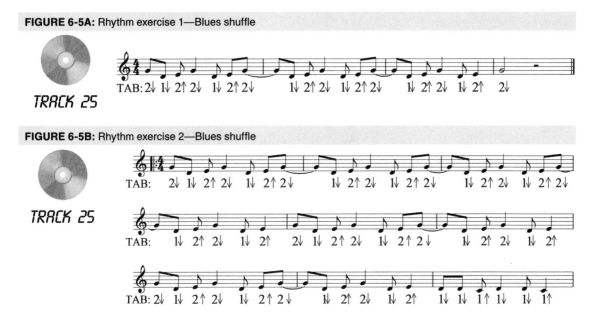

TRACK 25

FIGURE 6-5B: Rhythm exercise 2—Blues shuffle

TRACK 25

Melody and Chording Together

Combining melody and chords into one piece of music comes naturally for the harmonica. The design of the instrument is set up to facilitate playing chords on the lower end while making it easy to play scales on the upper end. This technique is also one of the most interesting and dynamic approaches to playing the harmonica, allowing the instrument to function in the roles of stand-alone accompaniment or as a powerful rhythmic and solo voice in a band.

Here's an example of melody and chording in the same song.

FIGURE 6-6: Melody and chording together

TRACK 26

Arpeggios

You'll recall that a chord is comprised of three or more notes played at the same time. An arpeggio is another way of playing a chord—but rather than playing all the notes at once, an "arpeggiated" chord is played by playing the notes in the chord one at a time in sequential order. Arpeggios can be played in either ascending or descending order of notes, meaning you can start with the lowest note and move up through the notes of the chord, or you can start with the highest note and move down. You can play an example of a series of C-major triad arpeggios simply by blowing holes 1 through 10 one at a time.

Practicing arpeggios is useful for improving your dexterity on the harmonica, and arpeggios also provide a good place to start when looking for notes to use in a solo over a chord.

FIGURE 6-7: Arpeggio

TRACK 27

TAB:1↑   2↑   3↑   4↑   3↑   2↑   1↑

Chapter 7 will explore harmonica tablature, the easy-to-read special musical notation that was created just for harmonica.

CHAPTER 7

Harmonica Tablature

Musical notation is the language musicians use to communicate with each other. Over thousands of years notation has evolved into its current forms, which include the standard notation with notes on the staff; music "charts," which are a stripped down version of standard notation, with the melody on the staff and chord symbols written above; and the specialized shorthand just for harmonicas that is the subject of this chapter—harmonica tablature.

Reading Music for Harmonica

The term musical notation refers to any written system of communicating how to play music. There are hundreds of different types of musical notation, with major differences between the way music is communicated in different regions of the world and sometimes even between different regions of the same country.

The most widely used and accepted form of musical notation, used the world over, is *standard notation*, where all notes and chords are written on a *staff* of five vertical lines, and all the information you need to play the music—including what key the music is in, what the time signature is, what speed to play it, how loudly or softly to play it, and exactly how long to play each note—is precisely specified. Standard notation can be written for any instrument, and can be played on any instrument so long as the player reads it.

While standard notation is exacting and has strict rules, musical notation itself has no rules except that it has the ability to communicate to the musician what he is supposed to play. Many composers have invented their own forms of musical notation, some of which include color and shape to graphically express musical instructions and look more like modern art than music!

Over time musicians have modified standard notation into more convenient forms, including:

- The lead sheet, which most people know as "sheet music," which is comprised of the melody line written in notes on the staff, with chord symbols above the staff and the lyrics to the song written below the staff. A chord symbol is a way of writing a chord in letter form, rather than as a stack of notes on the staff, such as "Gm7" for a G minor seventh chord.
- The chart, which includes the melody written out on the staff and chord symbols written above the staff, but no lyrics.
- The chord chart, which has only the chord changes of the progression, written as chord symbols, with no melody shown.

Musical notes themselves can be expressed in letter form, such as G or B♭, or they can be expressed as note symbols on a staff in standard notation, or they can be expressed in tablature.

Tablature is a complete departure from standard notation. Instead of communicating what note to play, tablature tells you where on your instrument to put your fingers—or in the case of the harmonica, your lips. Because tablature is based on a representation of the physical instrument itself, it is specific to one instrument, so harmonica tablature is completely different from guitar tablature or bagpipe tablature.

Besides telling which holes on the harp to use, harmonica tablature, or *tab* for short, tells you whether you should blow or draw that hole, and also whether you should bend the note or not.

FACT

The Pipeolion harmonica was designed in 1907 by manufacturer Christian Weiss. The instrument had ten brass horns protruding from the back with two reeds inside each horn. It remained in production for only five years, and it's one of the most sought after collectors' items on the market today.

You'll find that there are many different styles of harmonica tab being used by various people, and some styles look almost completely different from others. For example, some styles of harmonica tab use directional arrows to indicate blow or draw, while others use a plus sign (+) to indicate blow and a minus sign (-) for draw. Still others use a circle around the hole number to indicate draw. It's a curiosity that so many different styles of harmonica tab have been allowed to coexist because most other instruments have one dominant form of tab, and which is best is purely a matter of preference among players.

Even though the styles of harp tab can look dramatically different from each other, they are all giving you the same three pieces of information—which hole to play, whether to blow or draw, and whether to bend the note (and, if so, how much). And all diatonic harmonica tab has the hole numbers 1 through 10 in common. Knowing these things, you should be able to figure out any unfamiliar style of harmonica tab pretty quickly.

Tablature has advantages over standard notation, but it also has some big disadvantages. The main advantage of tab is that it tells you exactly where to play the indicated note on your instrument, whereas in standard notation there are no such directions. And because tab is based on a physical representation of your instrument you get more of a direct connection to the instructions than you would using the more abstract standard notation.

The biggest disadvantage of tablature is that it doesn't give you any indication of how long to hold each of the notes you're playing, so if you don't already know how the song you're trying to play goes, you'll get lost quickly. Another disadvantage is that you don't get the visual sense of the flow and direction of the notes, such as whether the notes are ascending or descending, that you do from standard notation. Furthermore, because tab is instrument-specific you can't use it to communicate with any musicians who don't play your instrument.

FACT

The harmonica has played a significant role in many films, both on camera and as a solo instrument on soundtracks. These include *Pot O' Gold*, which starred James Stewart as a harmonica player; *Shane*, which showcased a harmonica player performing a requiem at a funeral; and *Always in My Heart*, which prominently featured the popular Borrah Minevitch Harmonica Rascals.

But never mind the disadvantages for now. Harmonica tab is a great tool that's easy to learn and provides clear direction about how to move around the instrument, exactly where the blow and draw notes are, and where the primary bend notes are. The more time you spend learning songs from tab, the deeper your knowledge of the harmonica will become.

For the purposes of this book it was decided that arrows provide the best visual indication of blow and draw, and graphic bend symbols have been used for the same reason.

Counting

All music written in standard notation, on lead sheets, on charts, and in tablature shows the individual measures divided by vertical lines called bar lines, which are spaced fairly evenly across every line of music. In cases where tab is shown at the same time as standard notation—such as in this book—the bar lines may appear only on the staff and not be shown in the line of harmonica tab below.

You may recall that each measure in a given time signature has the same number of beats, as shown by the top number in the time signature. In order to keep track of where you are when reading music, you will need to count the measures as they go by. If you're playing in 4/4 time—by far the most common time in rock and blues music—each measure will have four beats, and will be counted 1-2-3-4.

FACT

There are many signature harmonica riffs in rock and roll that elevated the harmonica into the role of lead instrument, including John Lennon's opening of "Love Me Do," Sugar Blue's introduction to the Rolling Stones' hit "Miss You," the plaintive harp melody on Sting's song "Brand New Day," and Neil Young's opening harmonica notes on "Heart of Gold."

When you're just starting out playing over chord progressions, or when you're first learning a new song, you may find that you have to count all four beats of every measure to keep track of where you are in the progression. Once you're a little more familiar with the music you may find that simply tapping your foot on the 2 and 4 beats of each measure gives you enough grounding, and once you're very familiar with the music you probably won't have to count, or even think consciously about which beat you're on at all.

Hole Numbers and Note Names

It may be useful at this point, because both standard notation and tablature are shown in this book, to begin to associate the blow and draw notes of each hole on the harmonica with their letter names and their corresponding notes on the staff, as Figure 7-1 below illustrates.

FIGURE 7-1:
The 10 holes
with blow and
draw notes

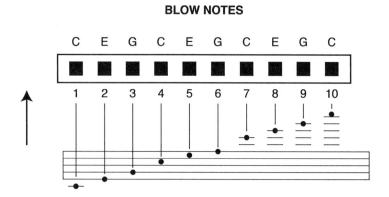

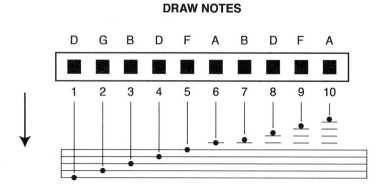

You might want to make a copy of this figure and keep it on your music stand or wall for reference until you know all the blow and draw notes on your instrument by heart.

The Arrow System

Another maddening way that different styles of tab vary is in their use of directional arrows to indicate a blow or a draw note. That's because some styles use an up arrow to indicate a blow note and a down arrow for draw. And, other styles use the up and down arrows to mean the exact opposite!

For the tablature in this book, an up arrow will indicate a blow note and a down arrow means a draw note as indicated in Figure 7-2 below.

FIGURE 7-2:
Up and down arrow symbols

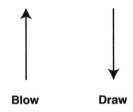

Blow   **Draw**

Air Direction

Bends

There are six types of bends that are included in the tablature in this book: a half-step down bend, a whole-step down bend, a half-step up prebend, a dip bend down, a bump bend up, and a double bend down. These bends are indicated in the tablature with curved arrows as shown in Figure 7-3:

FIGURE 7-3:
Bend notations

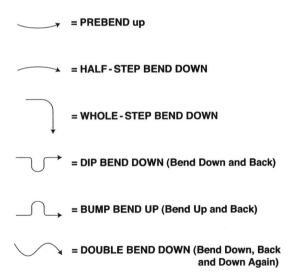

The one type of bend that hasn't been discussed up to this point is the half-step up prebend that's indicated in tab with the curved up arrow. Here's how that move is executed.

Start with your tongue in the already-bent position, and then begin your air with the articulation syllable "Duh." The note should sound bent, and then you allow it to rise back up to the unbent note.

Once you know how to bend a note, you'll also need to know how to maintain the bend. And once you have control of the bend and can maintain it, all you need to know to play a prebend is how to set your tongue into that bend position so that your note begins in the bent position—hence the term *prebend*.

Simple Notation

For the purposes of understanding the standard notation that appears in this book, here are the basic symbols and their meanings:

- The **clef symbol**, usually either a treble clef that looks like this 𝄞 or a bass clef that looks like this 𝄢 is the first thing that appears in the first measure and often appears in the first measure of every line as well. This symbol tells you what notes the lines and spaces of the staff stand for. Harmonica scores for standard diatonic harmonicas are always written in treble clef. If there were a bass clef instead, the lines and spaces of the musical staff would stand for different notes.

- The **key signature** is the next thing that appears in the first measure (and also often in the first measure of every line), expressed by one or more sharp signs or flat signs—one or the other. Because every key has different notes that are always sharp or flat in its scale, these sharps or flats tell you that those notes will always be sharp or flat throughout the entire piece of music, unless otherwise indicated. This saves having to write those sharps or flats in front of those notes every time they occur in the music, which makes the score much less cluttered looking.

- The **time signature** is the third thing that appears in the first measure after the clef symbol and the key signature. Expressed as two numbers, one above the other, the top number tells you how many beats are in each measure, and the bottom number tells you what kind of note gets counted as one beat. For example, in 3/4 time there are three beats per measure and the quarter note gets one beat. In 3/8 time there are three beats per measure and the eighth note gets one beat.

- The **sharp sign** looks like this: ♯. When it's written directly in front of a note it means that note is to be raised one half step above normal.
- The **flat sign** looks like this: ♭ . When it's written directly in front of a note it means the note is to be lowered one half step below normal.
- The natural sign looks like this: ♮. This sign is placed directly in front of a note when a note that's always supposed to be sharp or flat because of the key signature is instead to be played at its original pitch.
- A **dot** written after a note means that the note is to be played for half again its usual time value. For example, a dot written after a half note, which normally gets two beats in 4/4 time, which means it would now be played for three beats instead.
- A **slur**, which was discussed in Chapter 5, is represented by a curved line over or under a group of notes. Recall that a slur means that the notes are to be played together as a phrase, where the notes run together, as opposed to each note having a separate hard attack. Note that if a curved line is written between two notes of the same pitch, it is called a tie instead of a slur, and in this case it means you are to hold the note for the total number of beats the two notes are worth together. For example, two half notes (each of which gets two beats) of the same pitch with a tie between them would be played as one note held for four beats.

Try transcribing some songs in tab yourself. Start with a simple melody in C major. Figure out which hole you need to play for each note and whether it's a blow or a draw note, and then write it down in tab notation. This is a great way to learn how to play melodies, and it will help you perfect your tab reading too.

There are times in music when you're *not* supposed to play, and the musical term for not playing is, appropriately enough, *resting. Rest signs* tell you how long you'll be resting (as opposed to playing) within each measure. The most commonly used rest signs are:

TYPE	LENGTH OF REST
Whole rest	4 beats
Half rest	2 beats
Quarter rest	1 beat
Eighth rest	½ beat
Sixteenth rest	¼ beat

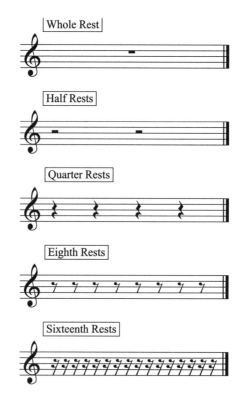

You're not required to memorize all this standard notation information in order to be able to proceed with your harmonica studies, but it's good for your musicianship if you're familiar with these basic symbols and their meanings.

Exercises for Reading Tablature

Here are five exercises you can use to practice your tab reading. Start slowly, taking however much time you need to figure out each note and work out each exercise, and once you have them down, speed up the pace at which you're playing them, all the time looking at the tab while you're playing. Soon you should be able to play music written in tab as quickly as you can read it.

FIGURE 7-4:
Tab reading
exercise 1

On Top of Old Smokey

```
T
A   4↑  4↑  5↑  6↑  7↑ 6↓
B
```

```
T
A   6↓  5↓  6↑  6↓  6↑
B
```

```
T
A   4↑  4↑  5↑  6↑  6↑  4↓
B
```

```
T
A   5↑  5↓  5↑  4↓  4↑
B
```

FIGURE 7-5:
Tab reading
exercise 2

Mannish Boy Riff

T
A   1↓   2↓   1↓   2↓   2↓
B   ↳   ↳

FIGURE 7-6:
Tab reading
exercise 3

Simple Gifts
(Single Notes)

T
A   2↓   3↓   4↑   4↑   4↓   5↑   4↑
B

T
A   5↑   5↓   6↑   6↓   6↑   5↓   5↑
B

T
A   4↓   4↑   4↓   4↓   5↑   5↑
B

T
A   4↓   5↑   4↓   3↓   2↓
B

FIGURE 7-7:
Tab reading
exercise 4

Simple Gifts (Chord Version)

```
T
A      2 ↓   3 ↓ (345)↑ (345)↑ (345)↓ 5↑ 4↑
B
```

```
T
A      5 ↑   5 ↓(63)↑(63)↓(63)↑(52)↓(52)↑
B
```

FIGURE 7-8:
Tab reading
exercise 5

A Blues Riff

```
T
A   2↓ 2↓ 3↓ 4↑ 4↓  4↓ 5 ↓ 5↑ 4↓ 4 ↓ 3 ↓ 2 ↓
B
```

The next chapter will look at how to play harmonica in the first three positions, the key positions on your instrument.

CHAPTER 8

Playing in Key Positions

Up until now the main focus of your training has been playing the harmonica in first position, with its simple major-key sound. While that sound is charming and has many uses, it is only part of the diatonic harmonica's capability. Learning to play in other positions greatly expands the types of chord sounds and chord progressions you can play over. In this chapter you'll learn the all-important second and third positions on the harmonica.

Song Key, Harp Key Tuning

Because diatonic harmonicas are designed to be centered around one major scale, you can't use the same instrument to play in every key like you can with a chromatic harmonica. This means two things: you'll eventually need to have more than one harmonica—in fact, more like seven harmonicas—if you want to have the ability to play in many different keys with other musicians, and you'll need to know which harmonica to select to play in any given key.

Choosing the right key harmonica when playing with others depends on both the song you want to play and the style in which you choose to play it. A folk-style or western traditional song would require you to play a basic melody in the same key as the harmonica, so you would choose a harp that's in the same key as the song you want to play and then play the melody in first position, which will be discussed further below. You may have noticed that the examples and the songs used so far in this book are all in the key of C and are meant to be played using *straight harp*, or first position.

FACT

Matthias Hohner, a German clock maker, turned his full attention to the manufacturing of harmonicas in 1857, producing a total of 650 instruments that year. Thirty years later the Hohner Company was producing over a million harmonicas per year, and today they make over ninety different models of harps.

A blues song or rock and roll song would most likely require you to play in *second position*, also known as *cross harp*. For that you must choose a harp tuned to the key three notes above the key of the song. For example, for a song in the key of G you would select a C harmonica and then play in second position.

Here's a quick reference about the correct harp for the key when playing cross harp:

C	D	E	F	G	A	B	harp
G	A	B	C	D	E	F♯	key

Any song that's in a minor key would require you to play in *third position*, also known as *draw harp*, and once again you would need a harmonica that's in a different key than the key of the song. For example, if a song is in D minor you would again use the C harmonica, but this time you would play in third position.

Here's a quick reference about the correct harp for the minor key when playing in third position:

C	D	E	F	G	A	B	harp played in third position
Dm	Em	F♯m	Gm	Am	Bm	D♭m	minor key

First Position

The term position refers to where on the harmonica the tonic (the first note of the scale of the key the song is in) is for the song you'll be playing. In other words, the note where you begin to play on the harmonica is what signifies the position you're playing in. For most players the useful positions are the first, second, and third positions, and those are the ones that will be discussed here.

First position, also known as straight harp, is the natural tuning of the harmonica and is played mainly using the blow notes of the harp beginning with the 1 hole as the tonic or key of the song. (Remember that the 1 hole and the 4, 7, and 10 holes are the same note but one octave apart, so those could be starting notes too.) Typically first position songs are folk songs or traditional songs associated with the harmonica like "Home on the Range" or "On Top of Old Smokey." These melodies will often be played using the second octave note (4-hole blow) as the starting point to allow room for movement up and down the pitch range of the instrument.

FIGURE 8-1:
First position
on harmonica

4 5 6 7 Blow

First-Position Licks

To play first position on the harmonica is to play in the key in which the harmonica was built. In this case you'll be playing in the key of C using a C harmonica. First position is when you play mainly the blow notes of the harmonica.

FIGURE 8-2: First-position licks

TAB: 4↑ 4↑   4↑ 3↑ 5↑ 5↑ 5↑ 4↑ 4↑ 5↑ 6↑   6↑ 5↓ 5↑ 4↓

TRACK 28

Second Position, or Cross Harp

Second position, also known as cross harp, begins on the 2-hole draw as the tonic or key of the song and builds from there using mainly draw notes. This would be the position for playing most blues songs that are in a major key. Be aware that second position relies heavily on the ability to bend notes to fill out the scale of the song.

FIGURE 8-3:
Second position
on harmonica

2 3 4 5 6 Draw

Second-Position Licks

In order to play cross harp, or second position, on the harmonica, your tonic note is always the 2 draw. On the C harmonica, in this case, it would be the key of G. Cross harp depends on mainly playing draw notes. So if the band is playing a blues in G, you should be playing cross harp on a C harp.

FIGURE 8-4: Second-position licks

TRACK 29

I want to play blues and rock—should I focus my practicing on second position?

Players who only practice second position often find it difficult to play any minor-key songs and will hit notes in a major scale that don't fit into the minor-key chord progression. They will also believe that they can't play many songs because they "Don't have the right key" harmonica. If you only practice one position, that is all you will be able to play, and you will be missing out on a lot of fun and growth as a musician.

QUESTION?

The reason shifting to second position to play a blues scale in another key works is that the resulting scale has a flatted seven rather than the not-bluesy-sounding-at-all natural seven of a major scale. For example, on the C harmonica when you shift to second position and start playing in the key of G, the seventh note of the G scale naturally becomes an F, because F is part of the C scale, while F♯ would be the seventh note of a G major scale.

Third Position

Before talking about playing in third position it would be useful to look at the difference between a major scale and a minor scale. You're already familiar with the C major scale, which is:

C, D, E, F, G, A, B, C

The *natural minor* scale, which is the most common minor scale, has flatted third, sixth, and seventh notes. Therefore the C-minor scale looks like this:

C, D, **E♭**, F, G, **A♭**, **B♭**, C

Note that it's primarily the flatted third and the flatted seventh that give the minor scale its characteristic sound, and these notes are common to all minor scales.

Third position, also known as draw harp, is used to play most minor-key blues, and it begins on the 4 draw as the tonic, or key, of the song. This position enables you to play a minor scale known as the *Dorian mode*, which has a flatted third and a flatted seventh (but no flatted sixth as in the natural minor).

FACT

Modes are classical scales that grew out of ancient Greek music. They are centered around the notes of a C major scale, and each of the seven modes uses the same consecutive notes of that C major scale—but each mode begins on a different note of that scale. This means that in each mode the half steps and whole steps fall in different places, which is what gives each mode its unique sound.

As with second position, you will need to be able to bend notes to be able to have a full range of additional notes to play, but mostly you will play on the 4, 5, 6, and 7 holes.

FIGURE 8-5:
Third position
on harmonica

4 5 6 7 Draw

Third-Position Licks

In order to play third position on the harmonica the 4, 5, 6, and 7 holes draw will allow you to play in a minor key. In the case of the C harmonica this would be D minor. Once again, if the band is playing in D minor and you wish to play along on your C harp, you would use third position, or holes 4, 5, 6, and 7 draw.

FIGURE 8-6: Third-position licks

TRACK 30

It's important to know that, whichever position you play in, you will need to be aware of the key of the song you are playing. From picking the right harmonica for the job to knowing whether you're playing in a major or a minor key and which notes are in the scale of that key, giving your playing this level of attention will improve your ability to play harmonica solos that make sense over the chord progressions you're working with. In addition, being aware of some of these simple rules of music theory will help you express your musical ideas verbally to other musicians, and to understand what they are talking about when they try to communicate with you.

More Positions

There are actually, technically speaking, twelve possible positions on the diatonic harmonica because it is technically possible, through the use of bending, blow bends, and overblows, to play all twelve notes of the chromatic scale on a diatonic harp. But this is very difficult and rarely done.

FACT

Harmonicas have come in some unusual shapes besides the normal linear layout. The Mira harmonica made by German maker Andreas Koch was a four-sided instrument with the four harmonicas mounted around a central cylinder called a horn-resonator. Koch also made the "U9 harmonica" in the shape of a World War I submarine. And the "American Marksman" harmonica came in the shape of a pistol.

The other two positions that are commonly used are fourth position and fifth position. *Fourth position* begins on the 6 draw and enables you to play a natural minor scale in A when played on a C diatonic harmonica. You'll recall from above that the natural minor scale is the one with a flatted third, sixth, and seventh. *Fifth position* begins on the 5 blow and enables you to play another type of minor scale known as the *Phrygian mode*, which has a flatted second in addition to a flatted sixth and seventh.

Playing harmonica in the various positions is a huge boost to understanding the complexities of the instrument. Eventually you'll grasp how all the notes on the harp and the bends and overblows that are available on each note fit together into the marvelous puzzle that is the diatonic harmonica.

The next chapter will go back to first position and study how to play single note melodies on the harmonica.

CHAPTER 9

Songs You Can Play
in First Position

The great thing about a harmonica is that usually one can start playing songs right off the bat with only a little know-how. The Richter tuning ensures that you'll get nice-sounding chords anywhere up and down the ten holes of the diatonic harmonica, whether blowing or drawing the notes, and the unbent single notes you pick out also fit right into the scale. Now it's time to take control of the single-note techniques you learned in Chapter 4 and use them to play exact melody lines on your instrument.

Playing Melody

A melody is defined as a succession of single notes assembled to form a purposeful sequence. What's the purpose? It's to inspire an emotional response in the listener. Whether the emotion is despair, joy, loneliness, love, or anything else, every melody ever written was meant to inspire an emotional reaction.

As a musician your job is to convey the emotion of your melody with expressive playing. The way you do that is to focus emotion into your playing while you're doing it. This means that you don't just play one note after another and congratulate yourself when you make it to the end—you listen to and interpret what the melody conveys to you emotionally, and then you put that feeling back into your playing when you play the melody to pass the emotional content along to the listener. Even a total non-musician can tell the difference between a song played mechanically and one played with feeling.

Coughing can be a problem when you're playing the harmonica. Before a performance it might be useful to coat your throat, like a singer sometimes does, using cough lozenges. This will help to prevent coughing onstage and can also help to reduce the effects of smoke in the venue if there is any.

The melody is the focal point of a song or piece of music. In vocal music the lyrics are sung to the melody line, and in instrumental music the melody is placed prominently above the accompaniment in volume.

Since the songs discussed in this chapter are probably well known to you, they will serve as a good measure of how well you can play at this point. If you can express the melodies well, then you are probably getting enough practice and gaining an understanding of the harmonica and its abilities.

Well-Known Folk Melodies You Can Play

Folk songs are by definition songs that have been passed on from generation to generation, which is why they're so deeply embedded in your consciousness. They're songs you've heard ever since you were a child, and songs that you'll probably sing to your own children. Elegant in their simplicity, folk songs employ few tricks or devices to get their point across, but rather communicate their well-worn messages of suffering and hope with simple, memorable melodies.

Here are five classic folk melodies to build your repertoire of major-key songs played in first position.

The first melody, "Simple Gifts," is an old Shaker hymn that expresses humility, faith, and satisfaction with life—all positive emotions.

FIGURE 9-1: "Simple Gifts"

TRACK 31

The second melody, "Tom Dooley," is an American folk song describing the imminent hanging of a man convicted of murdering his fiancé, so the mood is somber and resigned.

FIGURE 9-2: "Tom Dooley"

TRACK 32

The third melody, "Frankie and Johnnie," is another American folk song that deals with a man cheating on his lover and her consequently shooting and killing him, so it also expresses sadness and inevitability.

FIGURE 9-3: "Frankie and Johnnie"

TRACK 33

The fourth melody, "On Top of Old Smokey," is another classic American folk song. Although it's generally sung with mirth by children ("On Top of Spaghetti"), the song is actually about the heartbreak of losing a once trusted but now apparently false-hearted love interest, so the light-sounding melody carries a twinge of loss and anger.

FIGURE 9-4: "On Top of Old Smokey"

TRACK 34

Finally, our fifth melody, "Bill Bailey," is yet another American folk song that speaks of a lover gone away, but in this case the mood is almost comical, so the feel is light and humorous.

FIGURE 9-5: "Bill Bailey"

TRACK 35

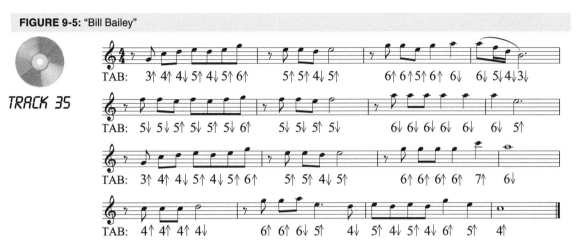

TAB: 3↑ 4↑ 4↓ 5↑ 4↓ 5↑ 6↑   5↑ 5↑ 4↓ 5↑   6↑ 6↑5↑ 6↑ 6↓   6↓ 5↓4↓3↓

TAB: 5↓ 5↓ 5↑ 5↓ 5↑ 5↓ 6↑   5↓ 5↓ 5↑ 5↓   6↓ 6↓ 6↓ 6↓ 6↓   6↓ 5↑

TAB: 3↑ 4↑ 4↓ 5↑ 4↓ 5↑ 6↑   5↑ 5↑ 4↓ 5↑   6↑ 6↑ 6↑ 6↑   7↑   6↓

TAB: 4↑ 4↑ 4↑ 4↓   6↑ 6↑ 6↓ 5↑   4↓ 5↑ 4↓ 5↑ 4↓ 6↑   5↑   4↑

Often you will find that a single note can be replaced by a chord or an octave to add depth, as on a song like "Simple Gifts" (Track 31). Once you can play these melodies with clean single notes, try playing them with chord melodies or using occasional octave notes played at the same time, and see how they sound.

E FACT

The *country scale* is a variation of the major scale that's often used in country and folk music for its natural bouncy rhythm. It's played by selecting the first, second, third, fifth, sixth, and eighth (octave) notes of the major scale. The scale is also known as a *major pentatonic* scale.

Chord melodies are created by playing the notes above and below the main melody note to create the chords, and they sound like a three-part harmony.

Dropping chords and octaves into your single-note melodies feels natural when you hear it, but it can be a little tricky to decide exactly where to use these effects. This is always the case when beginning to play, but it becomes second nature after just a little practice. Start by playing the whole song through twice, first using only single notes and then using chords and octaves to create a dramatic build.

Exercises for First-Position Play

Here are three exercises that will improve and refine your first-position play. First try a breathing exercise. More than any other position, first position demands that you be economical with your air because you're playing mainly blow notes. Try this: switch back and forth between playing a couple of single notes and then a chord. Make sure you're getting a full-sounding volume, but then focus on using the least amount of air pressure possible to maintain that volume. You'll realize how much excess air you normally use and how much longer you can play on the same breath if you're breathing from your diaphragm and conserving air.

This five-step tongue-slapping exercise will rapidly increase the accuracy of your tongue-slapping skills.

1. Using holes 4-5-6-7, play a single note on hole 7 blow while tongue-blocking holes 4, 5, and 6.
2. Switch to playing the octave holes 4 and 7 blow while tongue-blocking holes 5 and 6.
3. Play the whole chord 4-5-6-7 blow.
4. Switch back to playing the octave holes 4 and 7 blow while tongue-blocking holes 5 and 6.
5. Play the single note on hole 7 blow while tongue-blocking holes 4, 5, and 6.

Start slowly with each step until you can move from one to another cleanly, and then start speeding the exercise up.

Finally, here is an octave jumping exercise. Try this series of notes:

6 blow – 5 blow – 4 blow – 7 blow

The skill you're developing here is the octave jump from 4 blow to 7 blow. If you're not hitting the 7 blow cleanly when you jump, listen for whether it's the note above or the note below that's creeping in, and adjust the amount of your shift accordingly. You can also play this exercise using holes 3-2-1-4 and using holes 9-8-7-10.

Beautiful Is Better Than Loud!

When playing in first position most of what you will play are blow notes and chords. Blowing requires that you economize with your breath so that you don't run out of air in the middle of a place where you should be playing. If you tend to blow as hard as you can, two things will happen: first, you will make the harp sound forced and distorted, and second, you will blow out the reeds. This means that either the reed can become permanently stuck or, much worse, go out of tune. If you don't notice that you have an out-of-tune reed, it can be disastrous during play, not to mention expensive to replace.

The better approach to playing first position is to get the sound you want using the least amount of effort necessary. Notes played cleanly and with good breath control sound a lot better than loud, out-of-tune, or forced notes. The emphasis on clear, clean notes rather than loud ones is important because if you are unplugged, there are a lot of instruments that you simply cannot compete with for volume. This will make you want to play as loud as you can, and that will lead to some poor-sounding harp playing. If you are amplified, it is best to let the amp do the loud part while you just play it cool and stay focused on your clear playing. Let your amp create a desirable distorted sound, rather than distorting the sound of your harp out of fear of not being heard.

Lastly, you might find that on a song that has been played with a lot of volume and energy from the beginning, when it's time for the harmonica solo there's an opportunity for you to step up and play a soft, pretty melody to create contrast and bring the dynamics of the music down.

What does "dynamics" mean?
The *dynamics* of music are how loudly or softly you're playing. Dynamic changes are used to change the mood of the music. When the volume is loud, the energy level is high and the sound rushes over you, but when you bring the volume down, the mood becomes more relaxed and reflective. Dynamic change is a valuable tool you can use to express feeling in your music.

In today's music there's often a lot of pressure to be loud, and it can seem hard to compete against that trend when loudness is commonly equated with excitement. But just as you wouldn't want to eat the same food every day, hearing music at just one volume gets boring pretty quickly, and playing music at one volume only limits the emotional palette you have to work with.

Playing by Ear (Picking Out Melodies in First Position)

Playing by ear is the skill of being able to hear a melody, a song, or any piece of music and then being able to play it. Some people can hear a song just once and have the uncanny ability to play it immediately. For others it takes listening to a song ten times before they're able to reproduce it. If you fall into the latter group you're in the majority, so don't worry. Playing by ear is a skill that can be acquired with practice.

There are two components to playing by ear. The first is being able to listen to a song and remember what you heard, and the second is being able to find and play the notes you remember on your harmonica.

If you have any problem listening to a note and then reproducing it on your instrument there is a course of education called ear training that will help you. *Ear training* is a series of exercises that teach you this exact skill. You can find courses on CD that you can use to train your ear and develop this ability.

Play with Confidence

Part of playing any instrument is having confidence in your ability. This doesn't apply only when you're playing in front of an audience—confidence is even needed to play for just one other person. What's the source of this confidence? It comes from the knowledge that you've practiced enough that when you intend to play a phrase or song you know it will come out the way you intend.

Harmonica competitions provide an outlet for the gunslingers among you. At these competitions you stand up at a microphone and you have three to six minutes to prove to the judges that you've got it. The big competitions include the annual National Harmonica League in England and the Asia Pacific Harmonica Competition.

No one wants to believe that they will be scared to play when the time comes, but in truth most people are, especially until they have done it a bunch of times. Even professional players have moments of nervousness before a performance. Maintaining your focus and confidence will go a long way toward making it easier to play for people, and to eliminate this nervousness.

Chapter 10 will focus on how to practice effectively and how to set up your own practice schedule.

Practicing

The desire and drive to play the harmonica will fuel your way to becoming a good player, but practice is the road you take to get there. If your practicing is intermittent, random, and undirected, that road will be winding with lots of forks and dead ends. But if you make your practice habits focused and effective, that road can be an expressway to becoming a great player.

Why Practice?

If anyone ever forced you to take music lessons as a child when you had no motivation of your own, the words "go practice" can evoke terrible memories of mind-numbing boredom. Even skilled musicians who have practiced years have days when practicing is the last thing they feel like doing.

You're lucky to have the one thing necessary to make sure practicing won't be a bore—the desire to play the harmonica! When you're practicing something you really want to get good at, time flies by. You might wonder how musicians could practice for hours at a time. The reason is it can seem like minutes to them because they're so absorbed in what they're doing.

The hardest thing about practicing is sitting down and beginning. Before you physically sit down in your practice chair, anything and everything will distract you, but once you start practicing, all the fun of playing the harmonica will keep you entertained.

Furthermore, as you progress, your own improvement will become a huge motivator for you to keep practicing. Ultimately the goal is to push your skills to the limit of what is possible on your instrument—and then beyond!

Regular Times

Because simply beginning is one of the biggest barriers to practicing, it helps to have a regular time designated as your practice time. Factors you might consider when trying to figure out your optimal practice time include:

- The times of day when you have the most energy.
- The times when the fewest people are around who might be disturbed by your practicing, including family, roommates, and neighbors.
- The times when you're least likely to be distracted by other people, phone calls, and so on.

Having a regular practice time has many benefits. For one thing, it carves time out of your daily schedule to prevent conflicts with other activities. It also ensures that you will have the expectation of practicing every day. Try your best to practice regularly at your practice time, not skipping days but just practicing less on your off days. Aiming to practice for one hour a day is a good place to begin if you want to show rapid improvement, but even fifteen or twenty minutes a day is an acceptable place to start. You might even find yourself joining the five-hours-a-day crowd someday soon!

Get Organized, Be Prepared

Whatever amount of time you spend practicing, you want to make the most of it. For that reason it's important to organize your practice time and to create your own personalized practice routine.

One important part of organizing your routine is to make sure you allow time every day to get some practice in critical areas. This means you should work in segments where you practice scales, chords, tongue blocking and slapping, and whole songs you want to learn. As your technique develops you can add working on your tone, your vibrato, breath control, and other more advanced techniques. Make a plan for your practice sessions with a list of the things you want to work on, and plan your practice time so that at least a few minutes are devoted to each of these areas.

Another important part of getting organized is setting up a practice area for yourself somewhere in your house, or elsewhere, that's equipped with the following items:

- A comfortable chair with a back that allows you to sit up straight
- A music stand so that you can put your practice notebook in a place where it's right in front of your eyes without having to hold it
- A metronome for practicing scales and playing in time in general
- A notebook to keep your lists of practice routines, exercises, and other inspirations
- A tape recorder or other type of recording device to record your progress for self-evaluation
- A backup harmonica for those days when your own harp blows a reed or stops working for any other reason

Make a point of adding new techniques and exercises to practice to your list often, and go back frequently to refresh yourself on earlier material.

Relax and Focus

When you're getting ready to practice, it's good to take a few moments to relax your body and focus your mind. Chances are your shoulders, neck, and jaw are still carrying the tensions of the day, and those areas are precisely the areas you need to be relaxed to play well. Your mind is also likely to be full of the details of your day and will need a focusing exercise or two to remove those distractions. You'll want to be as relaxed and focused as possible to make the most of your practice time.

To unwind your body, close your eyes and consciously tell each area of your upper body to relax, like a check list: "relax your scalp, relax your eyes, relax your neck, relax your shoulders . . ." and as you do, focus on relaxing those individual muscle areas. This technique is very effective.

To focus your mind, you might start with the exercise of breathing through the harp that was discussed earlier—first breathe out slowly through holes 1-2-3, and then inhale slowly through the same three holes, listening as your breath is translated into sound on your instrument.

One more good exercise for focusing your mind on practicing is to think about *why* you're practicing—whether it's to sound as good as someone you've heard on harmonica, or to become a performer, or just to be able to blow people away who didn't know you'd been studying harmonica. Envision your goal while you practice. Hold it out in front of you like a carrot on a stick.

Finally, start your actual practice session by warming up with easy things that you can already play to loosen up your muscles and get into the swing of practicing.

Listening Is Practicing Too

One of the most important parts of developing as a musician is listening to a lot of music. It's especially critical to listen to other harmonica players, but any music you listen to has valuable lessons to teach you.

When listening to other harmonica players, check out their tone on the instrument (which is a function of their playing and their amplification if they're playing through a microphone—more on this later), the way they phrase their musical ideas, and the way they interact with their band. When you hear things you like, try to emulate them. When you hear things you don't like, avoid them in your own playing.

A narrower form of listening that's valuable is to listen for riffs you can "steal" and use yourself. "Steal" is in quotes because the borrowing of riffs is a long-standing and honorable tradition in music. The famous jazz guitarist Barney Kessel once said, "Borrow from one guy—that's plagiarism. Borrow from two or more—that's research." In fact, all musicians are the sum of their musical influences, and what makes each musician unique is that everybody's combination of influences is different.

When you find a riff you like and want to learn, listen to it over and over again until you know how it goes. Then slow the tempo way down and learn the riff at a tempo at which you can play it, speeding it up gradually once you know it.

Playing along with recordings is another excellent form of practice. It gives you the opportunity to play along with a band—often a great band—that affords you a very different and more lively experience than practicing alone with a metronome. There are even recordings that purposely leave out the harmonica part so you can play it yourself. The best-known manufacturer of such recordings is Music Minus One, but there are other series as well.

Note here that the music you listen to will be in a variety of keys, so you'll require a variety of harmonicas in keys other than C to play along. A good set of other harmonicas to start with would be an A harp, a D harp, an E harp, and an F harp, which will allow you to play cross harp for most common blues songs in the keys of E, A, B, and C, besides the key of G that you can play on your C harmonica.

If you already know what kind of music you want to play, listen to and practice in that style as much as possible after learning the fundamentals of playing harmonica.

Another tremendously valuable form of listening is listening to yourself play. This allows you to get outside your own head and body and hear what you sound like from the outside, from a listener's point of view. It's a great idea to have a tape recorder or a digital recorder sitting next to you when you practice so you can record yourself and listen back later to evaluate yourself.

ALERT!

If you're listening to a recording and you absolutely can't figure out what the key of the song is, remember that the key could be flatted or sharped, meaning that it's a half step off from the keys of any of your harmonicas. This is the case, for example, with many Little Walter recordings that are in the key of E♭ and require an A♭ harmonica to play cross harp.

Break It Down

The human brain can only absorb so much new information at one time, so if you're trying to learn a big block of new material you'll need to break it down into manageable segments.

If you're having a hard time learning a line or phrase, split it in half or divide it into smaller phrases that you can deal with effectively. Try to isolate the hardest parts or the ones you're having the most trouble with and practice them until they're as strong as any other part.

In fact, this is a good concept for your overall playing as well—if you're looking for large leaps forward in your technique, try making the weakest aspect of your playing the strongest one instead, through focus and concentration on that aspect above others until you are proficient.

Be musical in your practicing. Don't think of exercises as just a series of notes you have to make your way through. Instead, treat exercises like they're real music that you have to play with expression and emotional content—that's the way you want your playing to be, so it's what you should always be practicing.

Slow Down

One of the biggest mistakes musicians make at the beginning is to try to learn new music at too fast a tempo. Inevitably this leads to making a lot of mistakes, and by making the same mistakes over and over again you're effectively teaching your brain how to play wrong.

That's because as you learn new things you're building neural pathways, which means you're actually building new parts of your brain! Once you've practiced mistakes often enough they become ingrained in your mind by these new neural pathways, and they are much more difficult to correct later.

This is where your metronome comes in. It's best to learn any new scale, rhythm, or song at a very slow tempo to begin with, so that you can fully analyze it and play the notes cleanly with your current skill level. Playing along with the metronome ensures that you will be playing in solid, even time at whatever speed you practice. Once you can play the new material perfectly at the slow tempo, speed the metronome up a little and practice until you can play the material perfectly at the new tempo. Then speed the metronome up again. This process ensures that your technique will develop without built-in flaws. Your technique is built from the ground up, and a weak foundation will come back to haunt you later when you can't build advanced techniques on top of it.

There are software programs now that do what used to be impossible— they slow down the speed of music without changing the pitch, giving you the ideal situation for learning new, and especially difficult, pieces of music. One good example is the Amazing Slow Downer. Find it at *www .ronimusic.com*.

If you're playing a piece of music and you hit a rough spot that you can't play through without mistakes, stop and cut the tempo in half on your metronome. This may feel exaggeratedly slow at the time, but it makes it easy for you to play the notes correctly, and as you play them correctly you're building those good new neural pathways. Focus on the exact place where your mistakes are occurring, rather than going all the way back to the beginning of the piece just to work on your trouble spot. Once you can play the notes correctly, you can insert your clean, new phrase back into the piece at the original tempo.

Eventually these fundamental techniques become rote and you can stop focusing on them—they'll automatically become part of your technique and your muscle memory.

Muscle memory is a phenomenon where your brain and the muscle groups you need to play your instrument (including your hands, fingers, mouth, tongue, and throat) form a bond that can function while bypassing your conscious mind. Expert players have spoken of times when in performance they forgot an upcoming passage and, while their brain panicked, their body played right through the section correctly!

While your goal is to build up speed in your playing, it's not enough just to be able to play fast—you have to be in control of your technique at whatever speed you're playing to be a great player. Make sure that you're not practicing phrases faster than you can play them cleanly and correctly—perfect beats fast every time.

Evaluate Yourself Honestly, but Stay Positive

Studying music and practicing hard does not come without periods of frustration. You will have weeks where you're quite impressed with yourself for the obvious progress you're making. Then there will be those periods of time—even long periods of time—where you feel like you're making absolutely no progress at all. That's because you've reached a plateau.

Topographically speaking, a plateau is a large stretch of flat land raised sharply on at least one side above adjacent land. Plainly speaking, this means you've just completed a steep ascent and now you're in for a long stretch of level walking. And musically speaking, this means you've made a large leap forward in your technique, but now your brain and your muscles have been overloaded with new information and need time to absorb it before taking more on.

The fact is, you won't see obvious improvement every single day that you practice, and there will be long stretches of time when you wonder what the bleep your efforts are producing, since nothing seems to be changing about your playing. Be assured that there is light at the end of this tunnel. You'll wake up one morning and be able to play a riff that's been eluding you, just like magic. It's the interest on your deposit.

Your brain will always be ahead of your technique. This is true even for the greatest musicians. The unattainable goal is to be able to play anything your brain can conceive with perfect technical execution. And the fact that this is unattainable is a good thing—it means you'll always have something to strive for!

That's the challenge that drives you forward and ensures that practicing will never be a waste of your time.

Have Fun!

The bottom line about practicing is that it will probably become your favorite time of day—or at least your second-favorite. Bring an attitude of adventure and fun with you when it's time to practice. Invent little games to teach yourself new techniques.

When you're done playing your harmonica, always rap the instrument (with the holes pointing down) several times against your leg or the palm of your hand to eliminate excess saliva and anything else that might have gotten inside. Be sure your harp is completely dry before you put it away.

Here are a couple of final thoughts on the subject:

Follow your interests wherever they might lead you and you'll maintain a high level of inspiration and perseverance.

Practice being in the same frame of mind you would want to be in when you're performing—focused, concentrated, adventurous, inspired and musical.

The next chapter will enter a realm where your imagination and technique combine to take flight—the world of improvisation.

CHAPTER 11

Improvisation

Every time you see a lead guitarist or a blues harmonica player taking a solo, you're watching improvisation in action. The soloist steps forward and begins to play with no road map to guide her, allowing herself to be swept along by the rhythm and the chord progression until, in a stream of consciousness, a flurry of inspired notes emerges from her instrument. Even her band isn't sure what she might play next—this is the unpredictable beauty of improvisation. In this chapter, you will learn the basics of improvising without a net.

What Is Improvisation?

Improvisation is the spontaneous creation of music in the immediate moment, played without any written music or notation for guidance. Like forces of nature coming together, improvising musicians collide and bounce off each other, create force fields that propel each other, twist and turn and lead each other on a wild, unpredictable ride. The result is music that's being born before your very eyes, and it's a one-time experience that's never to be repeated. If your goal is to be here now and live in the moment, improvisation is for you!

Although improvised music is being created at the moment it's played, it often comes off sounding very organized. Great improvisation between musicians can come out sounding as complete and perfect as a painstakingly composed piece of music, where the different parts intertwine and build on each other to develop themes and variations between instruments that sound carefully planned and mapped out. The fact that such an illusion is possible shows you that real composition is taking place during improvisation. When you solo, you're composing music on the spot. There's even a saying that's common among jazz players: "Improvisation is composing speeded up, while composing is improvisation slowed down."

Studying the harmonica solos of great players and copying them is an excellent way to improve your playing and broaden your musical knowledge. Try breaking the solos down into manageable phrases and playing them slowly until you can play each one—then string them together into the solo and speed the tempo up gradually.

Being a great musician doesn't automatically mean you can improvise. Many highly trained classical players are not good improvisers because they've been trained their whole careers to read music and play whatever is put in front of them. When *nothing* is put in front of them they don't know what they're supposed to do.

Improvisation requires taking all the techniques and instincts you have developed as a musician and using them to navigate through the unknown, like a pathfinder riding a well-equipped wagon through uncharted territory. You don't know where you're going to end up, but you know you have the skills to get you there.

Components of Improvisation

There are many ways you can participate during ensemble improvisation. Each approach adds a different facet to the sound, and each requires a distinct set of skills on the part of the player.

Playing a Solo

Playing a solo is the first thing most people think of when they think of improvisation, because the person taking the solo is always the featured musician at the moment they are soloing, while the other musicians are taking a supporting role.

In simple terms, improvising a solo consists of listening to the rhythm and the chord progression that are being played by the band, and creating on-the-spot melody lines over those sounds. Improvised solos are scale-driven, meaning that the soloist must first know what key and what types of scales fit over the chord changes in order to improvise over those changes using notes that are appropriate.

When soloing over major-key blues or rock chord changes the go-to scales are the pentatonic scale and the blues scale, a close relative of the pentatonic. You'll recall that this is done by playing cross harp, or second position, and by playing a key of harmonica that's three notes above the key the song is in, such as using an A harp to play over changes in the key of E.

When soloing over folk songs or traditional music in major keys the scale to use is the major scale, using a harmonica that's in the same key as the chord progression. Remember that all the notes of that major scale are available to you when you play using holes 4, 5, 6, and 7.

When it's time to solo over blues, rock, or folk songs that are in a minor key you'll need to use a minor scale, which is played using a harmonica that's one whole step below the key of the chord progression (for example, an F harp to play in G minor), and by playing draw harp in third position.

Playing Accompaniment/Comping

While playing accompaniment to the soloist might not seem quite as glamorous as taking the solo, the role is equally important to the final sound that is generated by the band. You'll recall that accompanying the soloist is known as "comping," which is short for complementing the musician taking the solo.

The role of the players who are comping is to do everything they can to make the soloist sound as good and as exciting as possible. To accomplish this you want to play notes, chords, or phrases that not only enhance what the soloist is playing, but also raise the soloist's level of excitement in order to spur her on to greater heights in her solo.

Comping on the harmonica poses a particular set of challenges. Because the harp is usually positioned as a soloing instrument, if you start to play during somebody else's solo you tend to draw attention away from the solo—a no-no, because it's also very important in comping not to play anything that distracts attention from the soloist. But there are still ways the harmonica can comp effectively.

Some excellent tools for learning to play ensemble with other musicians are "jam tracks," which are special recordings that leave room for you to be the harmonica player. A good place to start is with the Mel Bay *Blues Harmonica Jam Tracks and Soloing Concepts #1* which is a CD that comes with a book of lessons from harmonica whiz David Barrett. There is a book two for the more advanced.

One way is to find a pattern to accent the rhythm while playing short staccato chords. The term *staccato* means to hold a note or chord for as short a duration as possible, like a short burst of sound. This is the opposite of notes written with a slur, which are intended to be strung together into one smooth sound—staccato notes are meant to be choppy and detached from one another. As an example, the harp might play short staccato accent chords on beats 2 and 4 of the measure, doubling the same chords that are being played in the chord progression.

Another way the harmonica can comp is to pick a note or chord and hold it for a long, extended time to create an organ-like background to the chord progression.

These are by no means the only ways for the harmonica to comp, so spend some time thinking of other ways you can make yourself effective, as well as listening to recordings to see how other harp players function under those circumstances.

Adding a Sectional Part or Rhythmic Accents

Another option when comping is to introduce a whole new part or feel to the music, as if you were adding a horn-section part. One example of this is to add a short, repeating chord phrase on every fourth measure of a 12-bar blues, such as:

1	2	and	3	4	count
1-2-3 draw	1-2-3 draw	2-3-4 blow	1-2-3 draw	(rest)	phrase

A sectional part like this repeating chord phrase adds excitement to the chord progression and also provides a rhythmic kick into the first measure of every line.

Rhythmic Alterations or Overlays

Still another way to go when comping is to add a rhythmic alteration or overlay to the existing rhythm. A rhythmic alteration would be something like adding a strong accent to one of the existing beats of the rhythm, such as accenting beats 2 and 4 of each measure. A rhythmic overlay would involve playing a separate new rhythm over the existing rhythm to form a polyrhythm. A *polyrhythm* is two or more rhythms being played at the same time. An example would be playing a triplet feel over straight 4/4 time, so that you were playing three beats for every beat of the 4/4 measure. Either of these approaches adds to the rhythmic interest of the music and provides the soloist with more options to play off of.

Phrasing

In music the term phrasing refers to the way notes are articulated and assembled into groups. A phrase is a group of notes that expresses a musical thought or idea. If a solo is likened to a paragraph of writing, a phrase would be one sentence of that paragraph.

Phrasing encompasses many factors that affect the way notes are delivered, including speeding up and slowing down, playing notes loudly or softly, accenting certain notes, the attack of each note, and more.

Another aspect of phrasing is where you choose to begin and end your phrases. If you phrase *on the bar*, you would begin your phrase on beat 1 of a measure and end it close to beat 4 of a measure. Or you could phrase *across the bar*, which means your phrase would begin somewhere in the middle of a measure and end either in the middle or at the end of a measure.

When you play a solo you're putting together phrases, or musical ideas, that begin somewhere, progress in some direction, and wrap up at the end with a sense of conclusion.

Roots and Fifths

When you're improvising over chord changes, you can get a lot of clues about which notes to play from the chords themselves. To help you do this, it is useful to understand how chords are structured.

Every chord has a *root*, a *third*, and a *fifth*. These terms refer to the *scale degree*; that is, the notes that appear at the first, third, and fifth places on the scale form the chord. If you're looking at the key of G, the scale degrees would be:

G	A	B	C	D	E	F♯	G	A	B	C	D...	note
1	2	3	4	5	6	7	8	9	10	11	12...	scale degree

Here is the way three of the types of chords already discussed in this book are structured and what the notes are in the key of G:

Major chord	1-3-5	G-B-D
Minor chord	1-♭3-5	G-B♭-D
Seventh chord	1-3-5-♭7	G-B-D-F (the F♯ of the G-major scale is flatted to an F natural)

Note that the common factor between all three chord types is that they all share the same root and fifth notes. This means that the root and the fifth are two notes that will appear and be the same exact notes in any chord with the same letter name. And that means they are both go-to notes you can play over virtually any chord. Bass players rely heavily on roots and fifths to create their bass lines for this very reason.

If you're trying to figure out what the root of a chord is, you don't have to look far—it's the same as the name of the chord. The root of a C-major chord is C, the root of an E7 chord is E, and so on.

When you're going to improvise over a chord progression, before you begin take a moment to identify the roots and fifths of the chords in the progression, and then find those notes on your harmonica. This will give you a structure of notes on which you can build your solo.

You may have heard musicians talking about a 1-4-5 blues progression. The numbers 1, 4, and 5 refer to the notes of the scale you are playing in. You are playing in the key of G in the following examples of 12-bar blues, so the notes of the scale are G, A, B, C, D, E, F♯, and G. The fourth note of the scale is C, the fifth note is D, so the chords of your 1-4-5 progression will be G, C, and D. Now you'll hear a G, a C, and a D on the C harmonica.

FIGURE 11-1: Roots, fourths, and fifths

TAB: 3↑   1↑   1↓

TRACK 36

12-Bar Blues

When musicians who have never met before get together to play they might come from wildly various musical backgrounds, age groups, and cultural backgrounds, but there is one progression that transcends all these barriers and unites musicians everywhere—the 12-bar blues progression. That's because the 12-bar blues progression is so elemental that most musicians, regardless of their age, background, or level of proficiency, know it—so you need to know it too.

The 12-bar blues progression, like all chord progressions, is based on the notes of the scale of the key the progression is in. The chords, like the individual notes of the scale, are also known as *scale degrees*, and they are often indicated in music with Roman numerals. For example, if you're playing a blues in G, the scale degrees would be:

G	A	B	C	D	E	F	G	note
I	II	III	IV	V	VI	VII	VIII	scale degree

The 12-bar blues progression is the same as the 1-4-5 progression mentioned above, the 1, 4, and 5 referring to the scale degrees I, IV, and V.

The classic "wah" sound you hear often in harmonica music is created by cupping your hands tightly around the back of the harmonica and then opening the cup you've made. This effect can be used slowly to create a long wah, or it can be done quickly and repeatedly to create a tremolo sound.

The first degree of the scale is called the *tonic*, while the fourth degree of the scale is called the *subdominant*, and the fifth degree is called the *dominant*.

Here's how the basic 12-bar blues progression goes:

4 bars of tonic I
2 bars of subdominant IV
2 bars of tonic I
1 bar of dominant V
1 bar of subdominant IV
2 bars of tonic I   OR   1 bar of tonic I and 1 bar of dominant V

There are other variations of the 12-bar blues progression, including:

1 bar of tonic I
1 bar of subdominant IV
2 bars of tonic I
2 bars of subdominant IV
2 bars of tonic I
1 bar of dominant V
1 bar of subdominant IV
2 bars of tonic I   OR   1 bar of tonic I and 1 bar of dominant V

and

4 bars of tonic I
2 bars of subdominant IV
2 bars of tonic I
2 bars of dominant V
2 bars of tonic I

12-bar blues progressions also come in minor keys. The chords appear in the same order and for the same duration as blues in a major key, except that in this case the chords are all minor.

Here's an example of a 12-bar blues progression. It's a slow blues feel in the key of G.

FIGURE 11-2: Slow blues in G

TRACK 37

T
A
B
    4↓   4↓   4↓   3↓   2↓ | 2↓   2↓   3↓ 2↓ |

T
A
B
2↓ (23)↓ (34)↑ 4↓   4↓   4↓   3↓ 2↓ | 5↓ 5↑   4↓   4↓   3↓ 2↓   2↓ 3↓ |

T
A
B
2↓   2↓   2↓ 1↓ (23)↓ 4↑ | 4↓   4↓   4↑   3↓   2↓ 1↓ 2↑ 2↓ |

T
A
B
2↓   2↓   1↓   1↑ | 2↓ 3↓ 4↑ 4↓   4↓   4↓   3↑ 2↑ 2↓ 2↓|

T
A
B
1↓   3↓ 4↑ 4↓   4↓ | 4↓   3↓   2↓   2↓ 3↓ 2↓ |

T
A
B
2↓ 3↓ 4↓ 5↓ 5↑ 4↓ 4↓ | 4↓   3↓   2↓ 2↓ 2↓ ‖

Here's an example of a 12-bar blues shuffle.

FIGURE 11-3: Blues shuffle in G

TRACK 38

T
A
B
  (123)↓ (123)↓(123)↑2↓(123)↑(123)↓2↑ | (123)↓(123)↓2↓ 4↓4↓3↓2↓ |

T
A
B
  2↓(123)↓(123)↑2↓(123)↓(123)↑ 2↓ | (123)↓(123)↑2↓ 4↓4↓3↓2↓ |

T
A
B
  2↓(123)↓(123)↑2 ↓ 3↓4↑4↓ | 4↓ 4↑3↓2↓ 1↓2↑ |

T
A
B
  2↓(123)↓(123)↑2↓ 1↓2↓3↓ 4↑4↓ | 4↓4↑3↓2↓2↓(123)↓(123)↑(123)↑ |

T
A
B
  1↓ 1↓2↓3↓4↓ 4↓ 4↑ 4↓ | 1↓2↓3↓4↓5↓5↑4↓4↑3↓4↑4↓4↓3↓2↓ |

T
A
B
  2↓2↓2↓2↓2↓ 2↓2↓2↓2↓ | 2↓ 2↓ 1↓ 1↓ |

T
A
B
  (345)↑ (345)↓ ‖

Here's a 12-bar blues in the 1-4-5 progression, only with more of a jazzy feel.

FIGURE 11-4: Jazzy blues in G

TRACK 39

Tone

Usually when a musician talks about a player's tone they are talking about the quality of the sound that is being played. Each harmonica player's tone is unique because it is partially determined by the player's physical attributes as well as being affected by external factors.

Physical attributes that are involved include the shape of the player's nasal cavity behind his face and the size of a player's hands, which can affect the sound when creating vibrato or cupping the microphone.

External factors include the type of amplifier or microphone the player uses. Trying to get what some in blues call an "authentic" tone is accomplished by manipulating the external factors. For example, buying the same vintage amplifier that Big Walter Horton was known to have played through is an example of going for an authentic tone.

The best place to begin with amplified harmonica tone is to listen to the iconic masters like Little Walter, Big Walter Horton, and Sonny Boy Williamson II, and to try to match their basic sound. Qualities that are common among many harp players' tones are that they have a lot of mid-range frequencies; that they use a smooth, round distortion that comes from an overdriven, small tube amplifier; and that they use a moderate amount of reverb. Once you experiment and eventually develop the specific qualities in your tone that you like, you will have established your own personal harmonica tone.

That said, it is also important to be consistent with the type of music you are playing. For example, it would usually be inappropriate to have a heavily distorted amp sound on a traditional country folk tune, unless you are trying to make it an experimental piece or to make some musical point.

A harmonica player's tone comes from several places. It can come from the shape of his face, the shape of his mouth, the way he holds his throat, or the way he holds the harmonica. For instance, vibrato for a harmonica player is achieved in two different ways, either throat vibrato or hand vibrato. The first example you'll hear is throat vibrato and the second is hand vibrato. Hand vibrato is achieved by cupping the harmonica, then opening and closing your hand rhythmically to create the vibrato effect, similar to a trumpet player using a mute.

FIGURE 11-5: Tone vibrato examples

TAB: 2↑

TRACK 40

Ensemble Playing

Playing music with other musicians in a duet or group setting is known as ensemble playing. When you're engaged in ensemble playing there are many factors you have to pay attention to in order to make sure the ensemble sounds as good as it possibly can.

The first thing you have to do is make sure that all the players are in tune with one another to avoid unwanted dissonance in the music.

FACT

Dissonance and consonance are terms in music that describe the stability of tonality in the piece. *Consonance* is a sound where all the notes are in tune with each other and form a stable, pleasant sound. *Dissonance*, by contrast, is an unstable tonal quality where the combination of notes being played clash with each other and make the listener wish for resolution.

Although dissonance is a tool that's sometimes purposely used by composers to make the listener uncomfortable for artistic purposes, it's certainly not something you want to have in your sound just because the group is out of tune.

Ensemble playing requires a different kind of listening than solo playing in that you have to divide your attention between what you are playing and what all the other musicians are playing. There's a constant give and take occurring between all of the musicians that requires attentive listening so that you can use that information to guide what you are playing.

Some of the factors you'll need to pay attention to in ensemble playing are:

- **Balance,** which is the relationship between the volumes of the different instruments. No musician should be overly loud, even when soloing, to the point where they are making it hard to hear the other musicians. At the same time, no musician should be so soft that the part they're playing becomes irrelevant or inaudible.
- **Style,** meaning the accepted practices of the genre of music you're playing. For example, you wouldn't want to try to play a folk song over a blues-style song. Different genres of music also have different general approaches used by the soloists in improvising their solos.
- **Chord progression,** to make sure the notes you're choosing are appropriate for the key and the type of scale being used. For example, if the band is playing a blues progression, it wouldn't work to try to play a solo using a major scale. You'll also need to know where the solos begin and end, meaning the length of one chorus, defined as one time through the progression.
- **Dynamics,** which is how loudly or softly the group as a whole is playing. It's especially important to be sensitive to where the music is going dynamically, and to make sure you're in fluid sync with the other musicians, because the dynamics of music play a large part in conveying the overall mood. If the dynamics are building to a peak, you want to be raising the roof in your part, too. If they're ramping down, you should lower your own volume and relax your feel as well, so that the group as a whole can make smooth dynamic changes.
- **Signals from the other musicians.** This is how musicians communicate with each other in the moment so that they can agree about where to take the music next. These signals might be quick spoken words, hand gestures, or even just the meaningful meeting of eyes.

This might seem like a lot of things to pay attention to at one time, but as you get more experience playing with others you'll find that your focus will expand to take in all these factors automatically and adjust for them as you go along.

Bandstand Etiquette

If you want to play ensemble with other musicians, it will help if you get an A for "plays well with others" on your report card. Ensemble playing demands that you pay attention to your fellow musicians and what they're doing and playing at all times, especially if you hope to be invited back a second time.

In Chapter 3 there was a discussion about times when it's best *not* to play when playing ensemble, which bears a brief repeating when discussing bandstand etiquette. Don't play under the following circumstances:

- When the singer is singing, except during breaks in the vocals.
- When someone else is taking a solo, except for possibly comping for them.
- When the opening or closing melodies are being stated (unless you're playing the exact melodies).
- If you haven't figured out the sound of the chord progression yet, or if you get confused about where you are in the progression during a song, then jump in when you get your bearings.

If you pay careful attention to your bandstand etiquette you'll be making a big contribution to the overall sound of your ensemble, as well as making yourself a popular player among other musicians.

Playing Along with Recordings

One excellent way to practice your improvisation and your ensemble playing at the same time is to play along with recordings. But before you begin to do that you'll need to know what key the song you're listing to is in so that you can select the right key harmonica to use. Here are a couple of tricks you can use to do that.

First, listen carefully to the opening chord of the song—way more often than not, that first chord will be the root chord of the key the song is in.

Second, pull out your C harmonica and check the sound of the opening chord against every note in the C major scale (holes 4, 5, 6, and 7) to see which one matches the key. If the chord doesn't exactly match one of those notes the song is probably in a flatted or sharped key, which will be a half step above or below one of the harmonica notes.

The next chapter will focus on the microphones, amplifiers, and effects boxes that you'll need to create the big, electric harmonica sound.

CHAPTER 12

Harmonica Gear and Accessories

If you're planning to play with other musicians in a band or other group setting, you're going to need amplification to be heard. But amplification isn't just about getting louder—different microphones and amplifiers have a major effect on your tone, which is the voice through which all your playing is expressed. This chapter will explore the microphones, amplifiers, and effects you'll need to get started

Microphones

A microphone has one job and that is to collect sound and convert it to electricity. While all microphones perform this function, they each have their own unique sound qualities that affect your tone. The following are some of the commonly available microphones you might choose.

AKG 414

The AKG 414 is an extremely sensitive condenser microphone that gives a clean, faithful sound with no distortion. If you're looking for an exact reproduction of your source sound, this type of clean studio mic is for you. The AKG 414 is currently available for about $950. The AKG 414 condenser mic demonstrates a clean sound.

FIGURE 12-1: AKG 414 condenser mic—demo

TRACK 41

Shure SM-58

The Shure SM-58 is one of the workhorses of the microphone world. This is the mic you're most likely to run across on stage at concerts or clubs because of its reliability and durability. Translation—these mics are hard to kill, no matter what happens to them. The SM-58 has a warm sound and will produce some distortion if the signal is loud going into the mic, which can be good for your tone. It is currently available for $100. It sounds like this

FIGURE 12-2: Shure SM-58 mic—demo

TRACK 42

T
A
B
12345↓ 5↑ 4↓   4↑   3↓   4↑   4↓   4↓   4↓   3↓   2↓   2↓   2↓

Shure 520DX

The Shure 520DX Green Bullet is the current model of the legendary Shure 520, originally manufactured by Shure from 1949 to 1977. After being discontinued for several years, the mic was reintroduced as the Shure 520D, made in Mexico.

Many of the Chicago sound players used this type of mic, and ever since Little Walter, Big Walter Horton, and Sonny Boy Williamson came on the scene, the standard for blues harp players has been the Green Bullet microphone, a high-impedance crystal mic. Originally these were army-issue microphones, which might explain why there were so many of them around. Later they were called into action as taxi dispatching mics because their intense reproduction of the midrange made them easy to hear over traffic noise.

The current version of the Shure Green Bullet mic is the 520DX model, which has many of the advantages and fewer of the foibles of the earlier microphones. The 520DX is less likely to feed back and, because the crystal has been replaced by solid state electronics, it is less fragile. The size and shape are also perfect for cupping the mic with the harmonica. The 520DX has a built-in ¼-inch guitar-style plug on a good length of cable. It is suitable for most amplifiers, and the new volume knob provides much better control of the mic while playing. It is currently available for $90.

Keeping multiple harmonicas organized can be tricky. Some players use a leather belt or bandoleer with pockets for each harp, keeping them in order by key and remembering the order for quick access. Or you can put stickers on them which are easy to read and can be seen in situations with little light.

As you will hear from the microphone demonstration tracks, there is a big difference from other microphones in the way a Green Bullet translates sound into electricity. When you play through it you may find that your whole presence becomes more focused on your playing because this microphone is made for this instrument alone. You can, and some people do, sing through a Green Bullet mic, but its true purpose is for playing electric blues harmonica. Many other harmonica microphones are out there, but none have the tried-and-true reputation of the Green Bullet.

The biggest disadvantage of the Green Bullet mics is that they are somewhat heavy when compared to other Shure stage mics. The 520DX Green Bullet mic, reissued from Shure, sounds like this.

FIGURE 12-3: 520DX Green Bullet mic—demo

TRACK 43

All three of these recordings of microphones are done without any effects whatsoever. These are only the sounds of the microphones themselves.

Other popular harmonica microphones include the Shure 545, which some players prefer to the modern Green Bullet for its shape, tone and power ($115), and the Beyerdynamic m160 double-ribbon mic which comes close to more expensive condenser microphones in its clean, flat response ($600).

Amplifiers

Equally important to your choice of microphone is the amplifier you select to plug it into. Amplifiers come in all shapes and sizes, and the amp that's right for you will depend on the purpose you're using it for. That said, there are certain qualities in an amp that are considered desirable for harmonica players. The first is that tube amplifiers are generally considered to be better than solid-state amplifiers because they have a warmer, rounder sound. The second is that smaller amplifiers are generally considered to be a better choice than large amps, both because they are portable and easy to carry and because their volume controls can be turned up much louder, which creates the smooth, distorted sustain that many players are looking for. Note that small amps might have to be amplified themselves with a microphone through a PA system to bring you up to the volume level of the other instruments you're playing with.

FACT

The unique sound of the harmonica is sought after even by those who don't play harp. Artists using sampled harmonica sounds include John Wesley Harding on his *Awake* album, Ministry on their song "Worm" from the *Houses of the Mole* album, and New York hip-hop producer Blockhead on his mix of "Sunday Séance."

The following sound demonstrations illustrate some of the approaches to amplifying your harmonica that are available to you.

Peavey Mark IV

A solid-state vintage Peavey Mark IV bass head with two fifteen-inch speakers is one example of the clean, big-amp approach, which has two primary advantages—it provides a very clean sound, and it provides a very loud sound. Bass amps have the advantage of not boosting the high and midrange frequencies that cause feedback, as well as emphasizing the desirable bass range of the instrument. This particular rig is quite large— the speaker cabinet takes two people to carry—but it's perfect for projecting loud, undistorted harmonica sound. Cost varies across stores and auction Web sites.

The microphone makes a big difference in your sound, and also your amplifier makes a big difference in your sound. The following tracks are examples of different amplifiers. The first is going to be a solid-state bass amp, using a Shure Green Bullet microphone.

FIGURE 12-4: Solid-state bass amp with Shure Green Bullet mic—demo

TRACK 44

$$
\begin{array}{c}\text{T}\\\text{A}\\\text{B}\end{array}\quad 12345\downarrow \quad \overset{\textit{tr}}{45\downarrow} \quad \overset{\textit{tr}}{45\uparrow} \quad 4\downarrow \quad 4\downarrow \quad 3\downarrow \quad 2\downarrow
$$

Fender Super Reverb

A Fender Super Reverb tube amp is an example of the mid-size amplifier approach. This is an all-tube forty-five-watt amplifier in a combo cabinet with four ten-inch speakers and built-in reverb and tremolo. This amp weighs sixty-five pounds, so it's moderately portable. It provides a loud, warm sound, and because it is equipped with a master volume control, it's easy to create a beautiful overdriven sustain that can be either loud or soft. It is currently available for $1,200.

The next example will be the Shure Green Bullet mic played through a Fender Super Reverb tube amplifier.

FIGURE 12-5: Fender Super Reverb amp with Shure Green Bullet mic—demo

TRACK 45

$$
\begin{array}{c}\text{T}\\\text{A}\\\text{B}\end{array}\quad 12345\downarrow \quad \overset{\textit{tr}}{45\downarrow} \quad \overset{\textit{tr}}{45\uparrow} \quad 4\downarrow \quad 4\downarrow \quad 3\downarrow \quad 2\downarrow
$$

Fender Blues Junior

A Fender Blues Junior tube amp is one of the most sought-after amplifiers among harmonica players, and is an example of the small amplifier approach. This is an all-tube fifteen-watt amplifier in a combo cabinet with one twelve-inch speaker and built-in reverb. This amp only weighs thirty-one pounds, so it's extremely portable. Because the amp is small it can be turned up to a loud volume to create overdriven sustain without being too loud compared to other instruments. The Blues Junior amp also has a "fat switch" that fattens up the bottom end of the sound and makes the overall sound rounder by boosting the input signal. It is currently available for $450.

And now what is probably the most popular amplifier used by harmonica players, especially in the blues genre today, the Fender Blues Junior tube amplifier, played with the Shure Green Bullet microphone. Notice that in the case of the two tube amplifiers, they both have their own distortion that is already part of the sound of the amplifier.

FIGURE 12-6: Fender Blues Junior tube amp with Shure Green Bullet mic—demo

TRACK 46

$$\begin{matrix} T \\ A \\ B \end{matrix} \quad 12345\downarrow \quad 45\downarrow \quad 45\uparrow \quad 4\downarrow \quad 4\downarrow \quad 3\downarrow \quad 2\downarrow$$

tr *tr*

Other popular harmonica amplifiers include the Fender 59 Bassman reissue bass amp, which combines the advantages of a bass amp with the advantages of an all-tube amp for another mid-size option, and the small Fender Pro Junior (a smaller version of the Blues Junior) and Fender Champ amps. Note that none of these amplifiers have built-in reverb.

Here are a couple of general tips about using an amplifier when playing harmonica. First, if you're using a guitar amplifier as opposed to a bass amp, you'll have to turn the treble and middle knobs down pretty low to avoid feedback.

FACT

Feedback is usually responsible for the sudden accidental high-pitched shrieking you've heard at events where microphones are being used. It's a result of a loop being formed where the microphone is taking in sound, amplifying it, and sending it out through speakers, and the resulting louder sound is then taken back in by the microphone. As this process is repeated the loud shriek builds in the speakers.

Second, the further you place your amplifier away from where you are standing with the microphone, the less chance of feedback you'll have. That's because feedback is created when the microphone is pointing at the speakers of the amp. Another good trick for avoiding feedback is to place your amplifier in front of you with the speaker facing away from you.

Effects Boxes

Once you've established your microphone and your amplifier sounds, you might want to add effects boxes to your rig to further alter your overall sound. For harmonica, the first two most sought-after effects that add to your sound are reverb and echo.

Reverb is short for reverberation, which is the bouncing of sound waves off of many different surfaces in an enclosed space at one time. If you've ever been in a large empty room and shouted or clapped your hands, you've heard all the "extra" sound that's left bouncing around the room after your original sound has ended—that's reverberation. Each of the many individual reflected sounds reaches your ears at a different time, which is why the reverberation continues after the original sound is gone.

Because reverb is often built in to amplifiers, it is not being looked at as a separate effect in this chapter, but be advised that reverb is also available as a separate effect if you end up with an amp that doesn't come with it.

Echo is the repeated reproduction of the original sound. If you've ever shouted across a canyon and heard your words repeated a couple of seconds later, you know what an echo sounds like.

Echo effects are created electronically using an analog or, more commonly, a *digital delay*. Adding delay adds excitement and three-dimensionality to your overall sound. What the digital delay is doing is making a copy of your original sound and then repeating it after a short delay, hence the name.

Echo can be added in a couple of different basic ways. Having just one echo that is placed very tightly against the original sound creates a *doubling* effect, as if two harmonicas were playing exactly the same thing. Having just one echo with a little more separation from the original sound creates a *slapback* sound, which is like the sound of an instrument bouncing once off the back wall of a room, giving your notes a concert-hall quality. The more space between the original sound and the echo, the bigger the "room" sounds. Having more than one echo repeat after your original sound is called *regeneration* because the output from the delay is being fed back into the input over and over again. This creates the sound of multiple echos that fade in volume as they repeat.

Note that the "feedback" knob is the one on digital delays that controls the number of repeats of the echo.

FACT

The Trumpet Call harmonica made by Hohner in 1906 looked impressive, but that's where the allure ended—the five dramatic brass bells protruding from the back of the harmonica were purely decorative and had no effect on the instrument's sound.

One note of caution with digital delays—you have to be careful that the timing of the repeats does not interfere with the rhythm of the song you're playing. Repeats of your sound that are not in time with the rhythm will throw the whole band off.

The next track is going to try adding effects boxes to the setup with the Blues Junior. It will add a Boss Digital Delay.

FIGURE 12-7: Boss Digital Delay—demo

TRACK 47

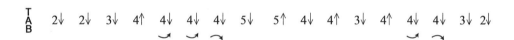

Another useful effect for harmonica players is *distortion*. You'll recall that turning small amps up loud produces a desirable distortion that is characterized by a smooth hornlike sustain. The amp is producing this sound because it is being overdriven by the high-volume setting. This type of distortion is created electronically by using an effect called an *overdrive* that produces the same effect by overdriving its own internal amplifier. If you're playing through a large amp that you can't turn up loud enough to produce natural distortion, an overdrive is the solution to getting the sustain you want at lower volumes.

Note that, although using effects to create this sound works well, a good tube amp that has a nice distorted sound and a good microphone will create that classic Chicago sound better than any configuration of effects boxes.

Using the Fender Super Reverb setup, the next track will add a distortion box, specifically the Boss Overdrive. This is to simulate the natural distortion you would get from overdriving a tube amplifier.

FIGURE 12-8: Boss OD-3 Overdrive distortion—demo

TRACK 48

T A B   4↓ 4↓ 4↑ 4↓ 5↑ 5↓ 5↑ 4↓   4↑ 3↓ 4↓ 4↓ 3↓ 2↓ 2↓ 2↓

One more effect that sounds good with harmonica is tremolo. *Tremolo* is created by running the volume control of the amplifier through a slow wave form that uniformly raises and lowers the volume at an even pace. This subtle wavering of the volume overlays the sound with a pleasant texture. Many amplifiers, including the Fender Super Reverb discussed above, come with built-in tremolo.

Now, there are boxes that will make tremolo sound, but nothing in a tremolo sounds as good as an old amplifier. This next track uses an old Gibson Skylark tube amplifier with built-in tremolo.

In general, smaller tube amplifiers are preferable. They overdrive easily and they minimize the problems with feedback.

FIGURE 12-9: Gibson Skylark amp tremolo—demo

TRACK 49

T A B   4↓   4↓   4↑   3↓   2↓   2↓

Customizing

Even after you've found your microphone, amplifier, and effects you still might be searching for a further refinement of your sound. Another avenue you can explore for this purpose is to alter one or more of the pieces of equipment you're currently using.

As far as your harmonica is concerned, options include retuning your reed plates or even replacing them with plates of an entirely different scale. Hohner makes a series of harmonicas known as 532/20 Blues Harp (MS) where combs, reed plates, and covers can be easily interchanged (the MS stands for "Modular System"), allowing you to easily customize your harp. Lee Oskar harmonicas are also designed to have parts replaced or interchanged.

Regarding your amplifier, the easiest modification and the one most likely to make a big difference in your sound is to replace the speaker. The speaker is the voice of your amp, and different brands and models of speakers have varying sound qualities. Some speaker manufacturers, such as Jensen, offer a "tone chart" that describes the differences in sound between their various speakers.

It's even possible to customize some microphones. The popular Green Bullet mics use microphone elements to pick up the sound. Different microphone elements have different sound qualities, and they can be interchanged inside the Shure 520 Bullet shell.

Cables and Adapters

Once you get your equipment to the location where you'll be playing, the next step is to get it all to work well in a foreign environment (read: not your living room). Here's a list of items you'll need to ensure that you're able to play when the moment comes.

- A microphone cable to connect your mic to your amplifier or effects. If you're going to be standing far away from your amp you might also need a microphone extension cable.
- A heavy duty extension cord for your amp. Most amp power cords are only about six feet long, and the nearest plug might be farther away. Also recommended—a couple of three-prong to two-prong plug adapters and an extra plug with screw terminals for your power cord for that wonderful moment when your plug gets severed right before you're supposed to begin playing.

- An extra fuse for your amplifier. Fuses don't blow that often, but when they do it's a show-stopper.
- If you play through a high-impedance microphone and you want to plug into a low-impedance PA system, you might need a direct box that accepts your mic's ¼-inch plug and comes out with a three-pin balanced output jack

Minor-Key Tunings

Harmonicas come in other tunings besides the diatonic Richter tuning and chromatic tuning. Some of the most interesting tunings are the minor-key tunings.

Lee Oskar offers harmonicas in two minor tunings, the natural minor and the harmonic minor scales. The natural minor is used to play straight minor-key songs, while the harmonic minor has an Eastern European or "ethnic" sound to it.

These minor-key harps are interesting because they blast you into a whole new tonal universe and break your head temporarily out of the diatonic tuning.

Bonus Track

Now you're ready for the next steps in your harmonica journey as you march toward mastery of the instrument. A good place to start is by checking out the essential recordings and the resources for further study that follow Chapter 15. Good luck!

We're going to end this chapter with a little improvisation for two harmonicas and guitar, played by your authors, Gary, Blake, and Douglas.

Blues improvisation for guitar and two harmonicas

TRACK 50

The next chapter will look at some of the legends of harmonica who paved the way to the highly developed harmonica music of the present day.

CHAPTER 13

Harmonica Legends

This chapter will look at a sampling of harmonica greats who changed the musical world and the way the harmonica was accepted as a serious and enduring instrument. The talent, dedication, and perseverance that these harmonica masters brought to their craft and to the stature of the instrument is inspirational. The accomplishments of these men and women redefined the instrument and gave it the prominence as a solo instrument that it currently enjoys. This is not a complete list of influential harp players, but simply an attempt to highlight a few of the harmonica luminaries who have paved the way.

Little Walter Jacobs

Marion Walter Jacobs, known as "Little Walter," is widely regarded as the most influential harmonica player of the 1940s and 1950s, and possibly the greatest blues harp player of all time.

He transformed the sound of the harmonica as it was known prior to him through both his electrifying technique and his innovation of using an amplifier and a Green Bullet microphone (now the most popular harmonica mic in the world largely because of him) to get a purposely distorted sound out of the harmonica. Little Walter's sound was smooth and sustained and sounded as much like a saxophone as like a harp. He also added the critical innovation of cupping his hands around the back of the harmonica, which added further to his distorted sound.

Little Walter was born in rural Marksville, Louisiana, in 1930. He left home at the age of twelve and went to New Orleans, where he began his professional career playing harmonica. A couple of years later he acquired a mentor in Rice Miller, better known as Sonny Boy Williamson II. In 1947 he went north to Chicago where he became a fixture on the blues scene and hooked up with his most famous group, which included Muddy Waters and Jimmy Rogers. In 1952 he recorded an instrumental piece called "Juke" that was released under his own name and went to number one on the R&B charts and made him a star. At that point he became leader of his own band, while continuing to record with Muddy Waters. And in 1964 he toured Europe with the Rolling Stones. He died in Chicago in 1968 after being in a street fight.

Big Walter Horton

Big Walter Horton, also known as Shakey Walter Horton, was a harmonica luminary said to be one of the best blues harp players of all time.

Besides developing a unique hornlike tone on the instrument and a completely distinctive virtuoso style, Horton was one of the earliest proponents of the amplified harmonica sound that defined Chicago-style blues, claiming to have begun using an amplifier around 1940. He was also a teacher and mentor to many players including harmonica icons Little Walter and Sonny Boy Williamson II and, twenty years later, to top players Peter "Madcat" Ruth and Carey Bell.

Horton was born in Horn Lake, Mississippi, on the outskirts of Memphis, in 1917 and moved to Memphis at an early age. He played with many of the top blues musicians of the 1930s era, including blues guitarist Robert Johnson, Big Joe Williams, and Ma Rainey.

After dropping out of the music scene for most of the 1940s, Horton came back big in the 1950s, playing with B. B. King, Eddie Taylor, and Muddy Waters (sitting in for Little Walter), as well as recording a large body of material for Sam Phillips's seminal record label Sun Records. Horton's most famous recording, which came out of the Sun Records period, was an instrumental track recorded with guitarist Jimmy DeBerry called "Easy," which became his biggest hit and is considered to be one of the best harmonica recordings of all time. Horton died in 1981.

FACT

The summer after Little Walter made his number one hit song "Juke" he decided to keep cool by having the doors removed from his Lincoln. Apparently he rode around like this until an accident with a center median caused the car to flip over—with Big Walter Horton riding alongside. The two got out of the car, flipped it right-side-up, and fled the scene.

John Lee Williamson, aka Sonny Boy Williamson I

John Lee Williamson, more commonly known as Sonny Boy Willamson I, was the first harmonica player considered to be a virtuoso on the instrument. The leading harmonica player of his time, Williamson forged the path that led to the harmonica becoming a lead instrument in blues bands everywhere. He was also a strong influence on two of the other top harmonica players ever—Little Walter and Big Walter Horton.

Williamson was born in Jackson, Tennessee, in 1914. He started playing professionally in the late 1920s and moved to Chicago in 1934. Beginning in 1937, he recorded as a band leader in his own right, and as a sideman with Big Joe Williams, Robert Lee McCoy, and Big Bill Broonzy, going on to record with Muddy Waters in the early 1940s.

Williamson recorded several songs that are still widely performed today. One big hit was "Good Morning (Little) School Girl," which became a blues standard that has been recorded and covered many times, including by Led Zeppelin, the Grateful Dead, the Yardbirds, and Ten Years After. Another of his songs, "Stop Breaking Down," is a blues classic that's almost equally widespread today. Williamson's blazing harmonica career came to a sudden and tragic end when he was murdered in Chicago in 1948.

Rice Miller, aka Sonny Boy Williamson II

Rice Miller did more than any other individual to bring the blues to a wider audience than ever before. He was the host of the first ever live radio show to focus on the blues, *King Biscuit Time*, a popular program that aired for over fifteen years.

Miller was born in Glendora, Mississippi, in 1899. He surfaced on the blues scene in the 1930s, appearing under the name Little Boy Blue. During this period of his career he played with the very top blues players of the time, including Robert Johnson, Elmore James, Robert Lockwood Jr., and Robert Nighthawk.

It was in the 1940s when, once in place as the host of the radio show based in Mississippi, Miller decided to simply "appropriate" (read: steal) the name of nationally known blues harmonica star Sonny Boy Williamson, aka John Lee Williamson. Because the latter never traveled to the South, this deception was allowed to continue until John Lee was murdered in Chicago in 1948. This is the reason for the number II after Miller's aka.

In the mid-1950s Miller began recording for the Chess label, where he was teamed back up with Robert Lockwood Jr. for a series of successful records.

Miller became very popular in the United Kingdom after appearing there on a folk blues tour in 1963 and started playing regularly in British clubs. During that time he played and recorded with a lot of rock's royalty including Jimmy Page, Eric Burden, and Eric Clapton. Miller died peacefully in Mississippi in 1965.

FACT

The King Biscuit Time radio show, first broadcast in 1941, made radio history by being the longest-running daily show in history. It's credited with creating new generations of blues artists, and later rock artists, inspired by the live performances of Sonny Boy Williamson II and Robert Lockwood Jr.

Sonny Terry

Sonny Terry was the most prominent blues harmonica player on the American folk music scene for over thirty years, He became known for crossing over from blues to folk music and blurring the lines between the two styles. He also introduced the innovation of using vocal sounds through his harmonica while playing, giving the instrument a unique sound.

Terry was born Saunders Terrell in Greensboro, North Carolina, in 1911. He was partially blinded as a young child, and another accident at around age sixteen blinded him completely. Because he needed a career that took his handicap into account, Terry opted to take up singing blues and playing the harmonica, having been taught by his father.

Terry first recorded with Blind Boy Fuller in 1937, and teamed up with his longtime music partner, guitarist Brownie McGhee, in 1941. The pair became popular on the folk music circuit, and, through relationships formed there, Terry began recording with folk luminaries Pete Seeger, Woody Guthrie, and Leadbelly. Sonny Terry and Brownie McGhee performed together until the middle of the 1970s. Terry died in 1986.

James Cotton

James Cotton has been a fixture on the blues harmonica scene for over sixty years. He is a crowd pleaser known for his powerful, hard driving, and energetic performances. Cotton was born in Tunica, Mississippi, in 1935. Before he was ten years old he was taken under the wing—and into the house—of Sonny Boy Williamson II, who became his teacher and mentor.

Cotton's first major gig was playing with Howlin' Wolf for four years beginning in 1950. In 1954 Cotton replaced Little Walter as Muddy Waters' harmonica player and stayed with him for twelve years, until 1966. Then in 1967 Cotton became the leader of his own band, the James Cotton Blues Band. A teacher in his own right, he has had many high caliber harp students, among them Paul Butterfield and Peter Wolf. Cotton continues to perform to this day.

You can find scores and tabs for some of Little Walter's biggest hits, as well as pieces by Big Walter Horton and Sonny Boy Williamson II, that have been transcribed by Glenn Weiser on his harmonica Web site. Find it at *www.celticguitarmusic.com/harppage.htm*.

Junior Wells

Junior Wells was best known for his swaggering bravado in performance and for carrying on the rich harmonica tradition of Little Walter and Sonny Boy Williamson II. He became commonly known as the "Godfather of the Blues."

Wells was born in Memphis, Tennessee, in 1934. In 1946 Wells's mother took him to Chicago, where he dedicated himself to breaking into the thriving blues scene, going from club to club trying to sit in with the biggest names of the day. His first major gig was with The Aces, featuring guitarists Louis and David Myers and drummer Fred Below. Wells joined Muddy Waters in 1952, filling the sudden void left by the departure of Little Walter. In the 1960s Wells teamed up with Buddy Guy to form a popular act that lasted many years. Wells also performed in later years with top rock artists, including the Rolling Stones and Van Morrison. Wells died in 1998.

George "Harmonica" Smith, aka Little George Smith, Harmonica King, Little Walter Jr.

George Harmonica Smith was a prominent blues singer and harmonica player who emerged on the scene in the 1940s. He was considered to be the leading chromatic harp player among the blues players of the time, and a leading proponent of using octave melodies in his solos. He is also known as one of the earliest experimenters with playing the harmonica through an amplified sound system, the first one of which he extracted from a film projector at the movie theatre where he worked.

Smith was born in Helena, Arkansas, in 1924. Although he spent a brief period of time in Chicago in the early 1940s he didn't interact with the Chicago blues scene, but upon his return to Chicago around 1950 he played with Otis Rush, Muddy Waters, and the Myers brothers (Louis and David). He went on to play with Champion Jack Dupree and with Little Willie John in the mid-1950s. After living in Los Angeles for eleven years, he moved back to Chicago in 1966 to rejoin Muddy Waters upon the departure of James Cotton. Smith died in 1983.

FACT

Alan Lomax, the famous folklorist who once said that folklore, music, and stories are windows into the human condition, got permission to go to the Mississippi State Penitentiary, known as Parchman Farm, in 1939 to record harmonica players Bukka White, Son House, and other bluesmen who called the penitentiary home.

Big Mama Thornton

Big Mama Thornton was a prominent blues singer, drummer, and harmonica player known for her gritty and energetic vocal style. In addition, she was the first to record two blues songs that made a huge impact on the American music scene. The first was "Hound Dog," recorded in 1953, which was a number one hit on the Billboard charts for seven weeks and was later famously covered by Elvis Presley in 1956. The other was "Ball and Chain," which she wrote and recorded in 1961 and which went on to become an enormous hit for singer Janis Joplin.

Big Mama Thornton was born Willie Mae Thornton in Montgomery, Alabama, in 1926. She first became known singing and playing with the Hot Harlem Revue, a band that she toured the South with for seven years in the 1940s. She went on to play with many other blues luminaries including Lightnin' Hopkins, Muddy Waters, Junior Parker, Johnny Otis, James Cotton, and Otis Spann. Thornton died in Los Angeles in 1984.

Jimmy Reed

Jimmy Reed was one of the biggest and most popular stars in blues in the 1950s and 1960s, and is widely considered to have been the artist that first drew large white audiences to blues music. He is best known for creating a large body of blues songs that, because of their relatively simple structures, became some of the most heavily covered songs in all of blues. This made him an enormous influence on the generations of players that followed. These songs include "Big Boss Man," "Baby What You Want Me to Do," and "Ain't That Lovin' You Baby."

Reed was born in Dunleith, Mississippi, in 1925. He moved to the Chicago area in 1948, where he played with longtime friend, guitarist Eddie Taylor. Together the two created eighteen top-twenty hits on the R&B charts in the late 1950s and early 1960s, a feat that no other blues musician of the time was able to reproduce. Unfortunately, Reed suffered from both crippling alcoholism and undiagnosed epilepsy, a combination that brought his meteoric career to an early close. Reed died in Oakland, California, in 1976.

Carey Bell

Carey Bell has been a major force on the blues scene for nearly sixty years. He is best known for his heartfelt blues vocals and for his blazing harmonica style that grew directly out of his association with some of the greatest harp players of all time.

Bell was born Carey Bell Harrington in Macon, Georgia, in 1936. He first played harmonica in a band with his godfather, pianist Lovee Lee, when he was just thirteen years old. Lee took Bell to Chicago in 1956, where he played with and was taught directly by harp icons Little Walter, Big Walter Horton, and Sonny Boy Williamson II. In the late 1960s he played with Earl Hooker and John Lee Hooker, and in the 1970s he played with Muddy Waters, Willie Dixon, and Hound Dog Taylor. In 1990 Bell was teamed up with harmonica luminaries Junior Wells, James Cotton, and Billy Branch to create the legendary album *Harp Attack!* Bell is still active on the blues scene today.

Paul Oscher

Paul Oscher wasn't hard to spot when he rose to prominence as the harmonica player for the Muddy Waters Blues Band—he was the only white musician in the band, or in any other major blues band of the time. Oscher broke the color barrier through his dedication to blues music and his skills as an accomplished harmonica player, guitarist, and singer.

Oscher was born in Brooklyn, New York, in 1950. He first started performing on harmonica at age fifteen, and by age eighteen he was selected by Muddy Waters to become the harp player in his band, one of the top blues acts in the world. Oscher played with Waters from the late 1960s to the early 1970s, and from there went on to play with an astonishing array of top blues artists including Otis Spann, Johnny Copeland, Luther Johnson, Johnny Young, Big Mama Thornton, Buddy Guy, John Lee Hooker, and T-Bone Walker. Oscher is still an active artist on the blues scene today.

The next chapter will look at the modern masters of harmonica who are the leaders in the field today.

CHAPTER 14

Modern Masters

This chapter will look at a sampling of the modern masters of harmonica, most of whom are alive and active on the music scene today. These are musicians who are driving modern harmonica music forward, stretching the boundaries of the instrument, and inspiring the next generation with their dazzling compositions, technique, and emotional content. Again, this is not at all a complete list, but simply an attempt to highlight a few of the players who are raising the bar and pushing contemporary harmonica music to new heights, leading the way into the twenty-first century.

Kim Wilson

Kim Wilson's unwavering dedication to the blues was the fuel he used to spearhead a revival of blues music in the 1980s. Both as the frontman of the popular Texas blues band The Fabulous Thunderbirds and as a solo blues artist, Wilson is responsible for a good deal of the advancements made in blues music from the time he entered the scene.

Wilson was born in Detroit, Michigan, in 1951, but he grew up in northern California, where he was exposed to and interacted with many top bluesmen of the time, including Charlie Musselwhite and John Lee Hooker. In 1974 he moved to Austin, Texas, where he met guitarist Jimmie Vaughn, and together they founded The Fabulous Thunderbirds. During this time, Muddy Waters had occasion to play in Austin, and he was so impressed with Wilson that he became a mentor to the young harmonica player. Wilson continues to be an active artist on the blues scene.

Billy Branch

Billy Branch is known both as a faithful beacon of today's Chicago blues style and as a sort of Johnny Appleseed of the blues through his innovative music education program Blues in the Schools, which has been in existence for over twenty years.

Branch was born in Chicago, Illinois, in 1951. Although he grew up in Los Angeles, he returned to Chicago in 1969, at which time he played in clubs and was tutored by harp legends Big Walter Horton, Carey Bell, and Junior Wells. Eventually he replaced Bell as the harmonica player for a six-year stint in Willie Dixon's band The Chicago Blues All Stars.

FACT

Need help deciding which top brand of harmonica you want to play? Artists who endorse Hohner harps include John Popper, Rod Piazza, Geneva Red, Toots Thielemans, and Mark DuFresne. Lee Oskar harmonicas are the favorites of Charlie Musselwhite, Paul Oscher, and, of course, Lee Oskar himself.

Branch has also played with Muddy Waters, Albert King, and Johnny Winter, among others, and was featured on the legendary 1990 recording *Harp Attack!* with Junior Wells, James Cotton, and Carey Bell. Branch is still an active force in blues today.

Rod Piazza

Rod Piazza is recognized for his searing harmonica tone and technical virtuosity that blends jazz phrasing in with blues technique. He is also considered to be one of today's top blues songwriters.

Piazza was born in Riverside, California, in 1947. He began his professional career at the age of eighteen in Los Angeles, with his own band as well as performing with blues greats Big Mama Thornton, T-Bone Walker, and Big Joe Turner. In 1968 he teamed up with the legendary George "Harmonica" Smith to form the group Bacon Fat, which performed and recorded for fifteen years.

In 1980 Piazza formed the Mighty Flyers with keyboard player Honey Alexander, a protégé of Otis Spann. The band, which is considered to be pushing the boundaries of modern blues music, continues to perform today.

Mark Hummel

Mark Hummel is widely known for his harmonica style that blends the rich tradition of harmonica greats like Little Walter and Sonny Boy Williamson II with a swing feel and jazz phrasing, a fusion of influences that is known as West Coast blues. He is considered to be one of the top harmonica players on the contemporary blues scene.

Hummel was born in New Haven, Connecticut, in 1955, but he grew up in Los Angeles. In 1972 he moved to Berkeley, California, where he performed with area musicians including Sonny Lane and Mississippi Johnny Waters. In 1980 he formed the Blues Survivors, a group that continues to record and perform today.

Annie Raines

Annie Raines stands out in the world of blues harmonica for one reason besides her formidable talent—she was one of the first women to rise up to the rank of highly respected blues harmonica player.

Raines was born near Boston, Massachusetts, in 1969. After studying the Chicago blues harp masters she made her own pilgrimage to Chicago, where she played with James Cotton, Louis Myers, and Pinetop Perkins. She also has played with blues guitarist Susan Tedeschi, Rory Black, and John Sebastian. In 1993 she met blues guitarist Paul Rishell, and the two of them continue to record and perform together to this day.

FACT

There are many different slang names for the harmonica that have emerged through the years. Besides the well known terms *harp* and *blues harp*, the harmonica has been known as the pocket piano, gob iron, band in your pocket, juicebox, tin sandwich, and the Mississippi saxophone.

Rick Estrin

Rick Estrin is easily recognizable by his rich, fat harmonica sound, his magnificent bending technique, and his overall dexterity on the instrument. He is also known for his excellent and prolific songwriting.

Estrin was born in San Francisco, California, in 1949. By 1967 he was performing in clubs in San Francisco. In 1969 he went to Chicago, where he played with Muddy Waters and Buddy Guy and worked with Sam Lay, Eddie Taylor, Johnny Young, and John Littlejohn.

Estrin formed the Nightcats in 1976 with guitarist Charlie Baty. During their early career the Nightcats backed up a host of blues legends, including Big Mama Thornton, Albert Collins, John Lee Hooker, and Gatemouth Brown. Now in their thirty-first year, Little Charlie and the Nightcats are still going strong.

Charlie Musselwhite

Charlie Musselwhite, along with Paul Butterfield, is credited with making the blues cross over into the much larger rock audiences of the 1960s.

Musselwhite was born in Kosciusko, Mississippi, in 1944. As a teenager growing up in Memphis he played with blues guitarist Furry Lewis. In 1962 he moved to Chicago, where he became a fixture in blues clubs, playing with Little Walter, Howlin' Wolf, and Muddy Waters. For years he also was the harmonica player for guitarist Big Joe Williams, replacing Sonny Boy Williamson I. Musselwhite also played with John Lee Hooker, Big Walter Horton, Johnny Young, Floyd Jones, and Robert Nighthawk.

Musselwhite eventually settled in the San Francisco area, where he performed with a who's who of the top Bay Area guitarists, including Harvey Mandel, Louis Myers, and Robben Ford. Musselwhite is still an active recording artist and performer today.

Gary Primich

Gary Primich was known for his dedication to the pure, old-school approach to playing blues harmonica, carrying on the rich tradition of Little Walter, Big Walter Horton, Sonny Boy Williamson I, and Sonny Boy Williamson II, while adding his own musical sensibility that made the classic approach sound fresh and modern.

Primich was born in Chicago, Illinois, in 1958, and grew up in Gary, Indiana. He spent his teen years studying the harmonica masters on Chicago's legendary Maxwell Street, eventually playing in bands that worked the street.

In 1984 Primich become disillusioned with developments in the Chicago blues scene that moved away from the traditional sound he loved in favor of newer trends in rock and funk music. Feeling that his opportunities in Chicago were limited, Primich moved to Austin, Texas. There he formed the group Mannish Boys with drummer Jimmy Carl Black. After two albums with that group he made two solo albums. Primich died in Austin in 2007, apparently from a drug overdose.

Charlie McCoy

Charlie McCoy is best known for his relentless work as a studio musician based out of Nashville. During his career, he has recorded on thousands of sessions with a dazzling array of music luminaries. Although he is best known as a harmonica player who paved the way for harmonica in modern country music, he also plays many other instruments including guitar, bass, drums, and trumpet.

McCoy was born in West Virginia in 1941, but he grew up in Miami. In 1959 he moved to Nashville, where he launched his studio career recording with Roy Orbison, and his career as a live musician playing with Stonewall Jackson's band. By the mid-1960s he was a sought-after studio musician, recording with Elvis Presley and backing Bob Dylan on four of his most well-known albums. Other top musicians on the long list that McCoy recorded with include Frank Sinatra, Simon and Garfunkle, Johnny Cash, and Chet Atkins.

Although he has curtailed most of his session work, McCoy is still an active performer and recording artist today.

Norton Buffalo

Norton Buffalo is known as a versatile harmonica player who is equally comfortable playing in the blues, rock, jazz, country, and R&B idioms.

Buffalo was born in Oakland, California, in 1951. He moved to Sonoma, California, in 1972, and then to Los Angeles in 1975, where he played with Commander Cody and, soon after, joined the Steve Miller Band where he remained the harmonica player for over twenty years, from the mid-1970s to the late 1990s. He also appeared as a studio musician on albums by Johnny Cash, Bonnie Raitt, and The Doobie Brothers.

In the 1980s Buffalo briefly formed a group with San Francisco–area musicians Micky Hart and Merl Saunders. Then in the late 1980s he teamed up with blues slide guitarist Roy Rogers to form a duet act. Following that, he formed his band the Knockouts, which recorded and performed for many years. Buffalo is still actively recording and performing today.

Mickey Rafael

Mickey Rafael is best known for his role as harmonica player for Willie Nelson, a position he has held for over thirty years.

Rafael was born in Dallas, Texas, in 1952. In 1973 he was invited to an informal jam session with Willie Nelson and Charlie Pride, among others. Nelson was so impressed with Rafael that he invited him to play a prestigious gig at New York City's Max's Kansas City, and the rest, as they say, is history.

FACT

Extraordinary harmonica techniques have been developed by players who pushed the envelope of what is possible on the instrument. Some of these include creating multiphonics (getting two pitches at once out of one hole by getting the blow and draw reeds to vibrate at once), bending the 1 draw *up* in pitch, and flutter tonguing (rolling Rs in your mouth while playing blow notes).

In addition to his longtime association with Nelson, Rafael has been a prolific studio musician, recording with U2, Neil Young, Elton John, Vince Gill, and Emmy Lou Harris, among others. Rafael is still an active musician playing in Nelson's band.

Adam Gussow

Adam Gussow is recognized for his roots approach to the harmonica, but also for incorporating elements of rock, jazz, and fusion into his eclectic harp style.

Gussow was born in Rockland County, New York, in 1958. He started playing harmonica in high school, influenced by artists including Little Walter and James Cotton. In 1985 he met guitarist and blues legend Sterling Magee, who was playing on the street in Harlem, New York, and who went on to become his longtime music partner. After a long stint together as popular street musicians in Harlem, the pair toured and recorded together for eight years.

Gussow was also notably featured in the U2 film *Rattle and Hum* in 1990. Gussow continues to play, teach, and write in Oxford, Mississippi.

Magic Dick

Magic Dick is best known for his role as harmonica player in the J. Geils Band. In that context and throughout his career Dick has been a force for the modernization of the sound and the role of the harmonica in contemporary music.

Dick was born in New London, Connecticut, in 1945. In 1968 he met John Geils and Danny Klein, and together with them he became a founding member of the J. Geils Blues Band in 1968. The band was together for twelve years and had a highly successful career of recording and performing.

Dick has played harmonica as a sideman for Debbie Harry, Patty Smyth, and the Del Fuegos, among others. He also went on to form a new group, Bluestime, with longtime band member J. Geils. The group continues to perform today.

Howard Levy

Howard Levy is one of the most outstanding harmonica players of his generation. In addition to his absolute mastery of the instrument, Levy is credited with the development of new techniques that dramatically expanded the musical possibilities of the diatonic harmonica, the most important of which is the overblow, which allowed the harmonica to produce notes never before available on the instrument. In addition, he is unrivalled for the number of different musical styles in which he can play fluently, which include jazz, classical, rock, folk, Latin, and world music.

Levy was born in New York, New York, in 1951. His professional music career began in Chicago, where he played with Tom Paxton, Steve Goodman, and John Prine, among others.

In 1988 he had occasion to play with Bela Fleck and the Flecktones at a folk festival in Canada, and in 1989 he joined the group, recording and touring with them for four years, a stint that made him widely known as a harmonica genius.

Levy has also played and recorded with a myriad of top artists including Dolly Parton, Jerry Garcia, Paul Simon, Jack Bruce, Laurie Anderson, Paquito D'Rivera, Kenny Loggins, and Art Lande. Levy continues to be a major force in the world of harmonica.

FACT

You may have noticed that women seem to be quite underrepresented among the artists discussed in this book, but there are a lot of great female harmonica players around today. Check out Trina Hamlin, Mattie Phifer, LynnAnn Hyde, Lady A, Beth Kohnen, Roxy Perry, Cara Cooke, and Geneva Red for a sampling.

William Clarke

William Clarke was best known for his original voice on blues harmonica, which combined elements of the Chicago blues sound with West Coast blues, and for his virtuosity on the chromatic harmonica.

Clarke was born in Inglewood, California, in 1951. He studied both diatonic and chromatic harmonica directly with George "Harmonica" Smith, with whom he performed and recorded for six years. He went on to record a string of solo albums that sold well and enabled him to tour continuously and cemented his reputation as a master of the harmonica as well as an excellent singer and songwriter. Clarke died in 1996, but his innovations on the harmonica live on.

Toots Thielemans

Toots Thielemans is the unrivalled master of jazz chromatic harmonica. Many people have mistaken his harmonica tracks for a brilliant jazz saxophonist with unlimited technique, because the complexity and dexterity he brings to the chromatic harmonica were unheard of before his time.

Thielemans was born in Brussels, Belgium, in 1922. Influenced by guitarist Django Rhinehart and saxophonist Charlie Parker, he developed a head for jazz that he applied to the harmonica. In 1950 he had the opportunity to join the legendary bandleader Benny Goodman on a European tour. In 1952 he came to the United States to live permanently. His first American gig was playing in Charlie Parker's band, and from there he went on to play with pianist George Shearing.

Over the years Thielemans has recorded and performed with the top names in jazz, including Bill Evans, Oscar Peterson, Ella Fitzgerald, Dizzy Gillespie, and Jaco Pastorius. He has also been active on the Brazilian music scene, playing with Milton Nasciemento, Gilberto Gil, and Luis Bonfa. Thielemans continues to record and perform to this day.

The next chapter will look at the stars of rock and roll who helped establish the harmonica as the popular instrument it is today.

CHAPTER 15

Rockers Who Popularized the Harmonica

This chapter focuses on a sampling of prominent rock and roll players who, either through their own harmonica playing or through other key efforts, brought the harmonica into popular usage as a soloing instrument in rock music. The pioneering performances created by these artists paved the way for the harmonica to become the powerful voice in modern rock that it is today. Of course, this is not a complete list, but simply an attempt to highlight some of the players who made outstanding contributions to the harmonica being accepted as a lead instrument in rock and roll music.

15

Mick Jagger

Mick Jagger, as lead singer of the Rolling Stones, is one of the most prominent and visible rock stars in all of contemporary music, a position he has
held for over forty years. Although not primarily known as a harmonica
player, Jagger has been a major proponent of the instrument in many ways.
He has played it on almost every Rolling Stones album and at every live concert (classic tracks with Jagger on harp include "Midnight Rambler," "Can't
You Hear Me Knocking," and "The Spider and the Fly").

But Jagger's larger contribution to making the harmonica a more popular instrument may be his relentless dedication to blues music, and to
bringing some of the biggest stars of blues harmonica to play on stage with
the Rolling Stones, exposing them to much larger audiences. Among the
harmonica greats to play with the Stones are Little Walter, Sugar Blue, and
Junior Wells. Jagger also appeared as a guest artist on harmonica on the
first *Living Colour* album. Junior Wells later paid tribute to Jagger by doing
a cover of the Rolling Stones song "Satisfaction."

Jagger was born in Dartford, England, in 1943. He is still active with the
Rolling Stones.

John Lennon

As songwriter, singer, guitarist, and founder of the Beatles, John Lennon is
one of the all time icons of rock and roll. As a founding member of the
Beatles, Lennon was arguably one of the most influential musicians ever to
inhabit the planet. The music of the Beatles transcended barriers between
age groups, races, national borders, and styles of music to reach the broadest audience ever reached by a musical group.

Lennon was also an avid harmonica player. Harmonica was the first
instrument he learned to play, and his harp lines have graced numerous
top Beatles songs including "Love Me Do," "Please Please Me," "Twist and
Shout," "Chains," "Thank You Girl," and "I'm a Loser."

Lennon brought the harmonica to the silver screen in the Beatles film
A Hard Day's Night with his memorable performance on the song "I Should
Have Known Better."

Lennon's power as a proponent of harmonica music is illustrated by the fact that Hohner went so far as to issue a special Beatles Harmonica in 1964, which came in a box with the Beatles' pictures on it, and included music to two top Beatles hit songs, a beginner harmonica instruction chart, and a signed photograph of the group.

Lennon was born in Liverpool, England, in 1940. He was killed by an assassin in New York City in 1980.

FACT

John Lennon was strongly influenced by another harmonica player, Texas blues rocker Delbert McClinton. While in the United Kingdom on tour in 1962 McClinton met the young Lennon, who admired McClinton for his famous harmonica riff on Bruce Channel's number one hit "Hey Baby." McClinton taught the riff to Lennon, who used it as inspiration for his own harmonica riff on "Love Me Do."

Bob Dylan

Bob Dylan is the best-known singer-songwriter in contemporary music. He burst onto the music scene in the early 1960s with lyrics so powerful that he became the spokesperson for his generation for years. Along the way he vhas influenced the direction of folk music, country, and rock and roll, bending all of those genres to suit his own musical vision.

The harmonica has been an ever-present part of Dylan's performances, and the image of his harp held in a metal brace around his neck is burned into the minds of music fans everywhere. He learned to play harmonica as a child and has pursued the instrument ever since. In fact, Dylan was signed to his first record deal with Columbia Records by producer John Hammond in the early 1960s as a direct result of his harmonica work as a sideman for another artist's recording session. He has incorporated the harmonica into every album he has recorded, spanning the many different musical phases of his career.

Dylan started out as a strong proponent of the first-position, major-key approach to harmonica, but once he came to New York City and learned to play cross harp he leaned toward that style as well as sometimes playing in the relative minor.

Dylan was born Robert Zimmerman in Duluth, Minnesota, in 1941. He is still active today as a songwriter, performer, and recording artist.

Neil Young

Neil Young has been a fixture on the music scene since the early 1960s. He first became widely known as a member of the band Buffalo Springfield, but it was after he left that group that his career really took off. Young released a series of extremely popular albums as a solo artist, and later hooked up with Crosby, Stills, and Nash to form one of the supergroups of the 1970s. Crosby, Stills, Nash, and Young's stirring appearance at the Woodstock music festival in 1969 rocketed the band, as well as each of its individual members, to international fame.

Since the beginning of his career Young has been a strong proponent of the harmonica, to the point that it's a trademark of the sound he's known for. He has featured it on many of his best-known songs including "Heart of Gold," "Helpless," "After the Gold Rush," "My My Hey Hey," and "Rockin' in the Free World." The introductory harp melody to "Heart of Gold" is one of the best-known harmonica lines in modern music. Young also played harmonica on the track "Furry Sings the Blues" on Joni Mitchell's popular 1976 album *Hejira*.

By his example Young has popularized the first-position major-key folk music approach to harmonica, and his harp parts are tabbed and studied often by those learning the instrument.

Young was born in Toronto, Canada, in 1945. He is still active on the music scene today.

John Popper

John Popper is one of the leading virtuosos on harmonica on the contemporary music scene. As the singer, harmonica player, songwriter, and founding member of Blues Traveler, Popper has been thrilling audiences for years with his dazzling and hyperactive harp style, a style born more from listening to great jazz improvisers than to the classic blues harmonica masters. His musicianship has pushed the harmonica to the forefront of soloing instruments in the modern rock setting.

FACT

As a high school student, John Popper ran in a student election. When his turn came to make a speech he pulled out a harmonica and started to wail. The crowd responded with wild applause and dancing—it was absolutely the winning performance. But instead of winning the election, Popper got suspended from school.

Popper has also been a leading proponent of the use of effects to create his harmonica sound, using devices including wah-wahs, fuzz tones, synthesizers, digital delays, and octave generators to stretch the limits of what is possible on the instrument.

Popper was born in Cleveland, Ohio, in 1967. He is still a driving force on harmonica today. His latest album is *The John Popper Project* featuring DJ Logic, released in 2006.

Sugar Blue

Sugar Blue is one of the most skilled and versatile instrumentalists playing harmonica today. His harp style blends jazz and blues influences propelled by his excellent technique and virtuosity on the instrument.

Blue grew up in the environment of the famous Apollo Theatre in Harlem, New York, where his mother was a performer. He learned harmonica as a child and was doing recording sessions by the time he was twenty-five. Blue met Mick Jagger of the Rolling Stones while living in Paris in 1976 and was invited to be a guest on the Stones' recording sessions for their *Some Girls* album. His well-known eighteen-note riff opening the Rolling Stones track "Miss You" from that album became one of the most prominent harmonica riffs in rock. He recorded on two more Rolling Stones albums after that, as well as touring with the band.

Blue went on to play with many luminaries from the blues scene, including Junior Wells, Carey Bell, James Cotton, Big Walter Horton, and Willie Dixon. He also played with jazz great Stan Getz, and in 1985 was awarded a Grammy for his work on a live jazz album from the Montreux Jazz Festival.

Blue was born James Whiting in New York, New York, in 1950. He is still performing and recording today.

Bruce Springsteen

Bruce Springsteen has been one of America's top rock musicians and song-writers for the past thirty-five years, over which time he has won an astonishing fifteen Grammy awards between 1984 and 2006 as well as selling millions of albums.

FACT

Bruce Springsteen was an admirer of the Dave Clark Five, one of the "British Invasion" bands that stormed American shores in the early 1960s with hits like "Bits and Pieces," "Glad All Over," and "Catch Us If You Can." Springsteen reportedly played the Dave Clark Five to his E Street Band and told them, "This is what *we* should sound like."

The harmonica has been an integral part of Springsteen's recordings and performances since the beginning of his career, and in many ways he has carried on the Woody Guthrie tradition of the American singer/song-writer/harmonica-playing guitarist. He has played the harmonica on every recording and in every concert, especially featuring the instrument on his acoustic albums including *Nebraska* and *Ghost of Tom Joad*. But even while carrying this traditional torch, Springsteen has also forged new paths on the harmonica, incorporating it into top songs in the loud, electric rock genre in a prominent way on songs including "Thunder Road" from the *Born to Run* album, "Promised Land" from the *Darkness on the Edge of Town* album, and "The River" from *The River* album.

Springsteen was born in Long Branch, New Jersey, in 1949. He is still recording and touring today.

John Sebastian

John Sebastian rose to notoriety on the music scene with his band The Lovin' Spoonful in the early 1960s. The group had a long string of top hits including "Do You Believe in Magic," "Did You Ever Have to Make Up Your Mind," "Summer in the City," "Daydream," and "Nashville Cats."

Blues harmonica never sounded so lighthearted and fun until it met up with the good-time music of the Lovin' Spoonful. Sebastian took the harmonica, an instrument often associated with broken hearts, turned the frown upside down and made it smile on top-ten pop charts all over the world. His happy blues harmonica instrumentals, like "Night Owl Blues" from the *Do You Believe in Magic* album and "Big Noise from Speonk" from the *Daydream* album, turned a whole generation of 60s kids on to the blues harp.

Sebastian also did a lot of studio work with other bands. He played on the Doors' song "Roadhouse Blues" from the *Morrison Hotel* album, on the Crosby, Stills, Nash, and Young tune "Déjà Vu" from the *Déjà Vu* album, on many tracks of *Tim Hardin I*, and on many other influential recordings.

Sebastian also brought his style of blues harmonica to film soundtracks with "Lonely (Amy's Theme)" from the Francis Ford Coppola film *You're a Big Boy Now* and to Woody Allen's *What's Up Tiger Lily?* for which Sebastian wrote the score.

Sebastian was born in New York, New York, in 1941. His latest recording, released in 2007, is *Satisfied*, a duet album with mandolin player David Grisman.

Stevie Wonder

"Little" Stevie Wonder burst upon the Motown music scene in 1963 with his debut album *The 12 Year Old Genius*. His first big hit was a harmonica solo from that album called "Fingertips—part 2" which became a number one hit on the Billboard Hot 100 chart.

Wonder was best known in his early career for his harmonica playing, and the virtuosity he displayed on "Fingertips" had a huge influence on harmonica players.

FACT

When Stevie Wonder's song "Fingertips" rocketed to the top of the Billboard Hot 100 chart in 1963 he became the youngest person ever to achieve a number one hit. Then, in 1999, he became the youngest person ever to receive a Kennedy Center Honor for lifetime contribution to arts and culture, which was presented to him by President Bill Clinton.

As his career went on he became the leading voice of harmonica of his time in pop music. His signature chromatic harmonica style (with slide-in as the home position) has become one of the most widely imitated sounds on that instrument. His joyous harmonica solo on the 1968 hit "For Once in My Life" is a shining example of his buoyant and lyrical approach to melody. Wonder was also driven to record *Alfie*, an instrumental harmonica album in 1968, but Motown declined to release it, instead allowing it to be released on another label with the artist listed as Eivets Rednow, a lightly disguised version of Wonder's name.

Wonder was born Steveland Hardaway Judkins in Saginaw, Michigan, in 1950. His latest album is *A Time to Love*, released in 2007.

Bob Hite

As lead singer and harmonica player of Canned Heat, Bob Hite was one of the most prominent harmonica players of the 1960s and 1970s. Known as "The Bear" for his large stature, Hite was a masterful diatonic harmonica player whose syncopated rhythms percolated over Canned Heat's signature boogie beat. The infectious energy the band created with their blend of blues and rock drew the interest of huge audiences to harmonica-driven blues.

Hite was born in Torrance, California, in 1945. He died of a heart attack during a performance in 1981.

Chrissie Hynde

As the singer, guitarist, harmonica player, and songwriter of the Pretenders, one of rock's most beloved bands, Chrissie Hynde is one of the most visible women in modern music today.

Hynde's scorching harmonica solos have graced many Pretenders songs, the best known of which is her solo on the Pretenders' hit single "Middle of the Road."

In addition to her considerable work on the harmonica with the Pretenders, Hynde also played harmonica with Bob Dylan and Eric Clapton at Wembly Stadium in London, England, in 1984 in a famous performance of Dylan's "Leopard-Skin Pill-Box Hat." She also appears on harmonica on Phil Manzanera's 2004 *6PM* album.

Hynde was born on Akron, Ohio, in 1951. She is still active on the music scene today.

Paul Butterfield

Paul Butterfield would be considered one of the greatest blues harmonica players of all time under any circumstances, but his case is made all the more special by the fact that he was the first white blues harp player to develop his own signature sound on the instrument and to have it considered legitimate by the black blues community. By doing so, he set the example that a non-black could be considered a serious blues harmonica player if he was dedicated enough and talented enough, and thus he cleared a path for other harp players to follow.

What's more, Butterfield's blazing harmonica style became a window through which large audiences of white listeners became attracted to blues music during the 1960s and 1970s, listeners who subsequently went on to explore the other icons of blues because of the rich experience they'd had listening to him.

Butterfield's most important albums were *The Paul Butterfield Blues Band* (1965), *East-West* (1966), and *The Resurrection of Pigboy Crabshaw* (1967).

Butterfield was born in Chicago, Illinois, in 1942. He died of a drug overdose in Hollywood, California in 1987.

APPENDIX A

The Essential Harmonica Recordings

Early Blues

Little Walter, *The Chess 50th Anniversary Collection: Little Walter—His Best*

Sonny Boy Williamson I, *The Bluebird Recordings 1937–1938*

Sonny Boy Williamson II, *The Chess 50th Anniversary Collection: Sonny Boy Williamson—His Best*

Sonny Terry and Brownie McGee, *Brownie McGee and Sonny Terry Sing*

Big Walter Horton, *They Call Me Big Walter*

Carey Bell, *Heartaches and Pain*

James Cotton, *Pure Cotton*

Junior Wells, *Hoodoo Man Blues*

George "Harmonica" Smith, *Harmonica Ace: The Modern Masters*

Big Mama Thornton, *The Complete Vanguard Recordings*

Jimmy Reed, *Blues Masters: The Very Best of Jimmy Reed*

Paul Oscher, *Alone with the Blues*

Modern Blues

Billy Branch, Carey Bell, James Cotton, and Junior Wells, *Harp Attack!*

Various Artists, *What's Shakin'*

Sugar Blue, *Blues Explosion*

John Mayall, *Bluesbreakers with Eric Clapton*

Paul Butterfield, *East West*

Paul Butterfield—"Mystery Train," "Mannish Boy," on The Band, *The Last Waltz*

Little Charlie and the Nightcats, *Nine Lives*

Norton Buffalo and the Knockouts, *King of the Highway*

Charlie Musselwhite, *Delta Hardware*

Adam Gussow—Satan and Adam, *Harlem Blues*

Classic Rock

Canned Heat, "On the Road Again" (single)

Black Sabbath, "The Wizard" (single)

Led Zeppelin, "When the Levee Breaks" (single)

J. Geils Band, *"Live" Full House*

Bruce Springsteen, *Nebraska*

80s and 90s

Eurythmics, "Missionary Man" (single)

Pretenders, "Middle of the Road" (single)

Neil Young, *Harvest Moon*

Blues Traveler, *Four*

Folk and Country

Bob Dylan, *Blonde on Blonde*

John Sebastian, *Do You Believe in Magic?*

Jazz

Bela Flek and The Flektones, *Flight of the Cosmic Hippo*

Howard Levy, *The Molinaro-Levy Project Live*

Toots Thielemans, *Only Trust Your Heart*

APPENDIX B

Resources for Further Study

Books

Jon Gindick and Barry Geller, *Country and Blues Harmonica for the Musically Hopeless* (Klutz Press)

Paul Butterfield, *Paul Butterfield—Blues Harmonica Master Class: Book/CD Pack* (Homespun-Pap/Com)

Magazines

Mel Bay Harmonica Sessions—monthly online magazine
www.harmonicasessions.com/index.html

Southwest Blues Magazine—monthly online magazine
www.southwestblues.com/home.htm

Videos/DVDs

John Sebastian, *John Sebastian Teaches Blues Harmonica* (Homespun)

Peter Madcat Ruth, *Anyone Can Play Harmonica: An Easy Guide to Getting Started* (Homespun)

Norton Buffalo, *Harmonica Power! Norton Buffalo's Blues Techniques* (Homespun)

Web sites

www.hohnerusa.com
The Hohner Web site—click on "Instruments" and "Harmonicas" to get to the good stuff!

www.hunterharp.com/harplink.htm
Good portal to harmonica Web sites of all kinds, including artist sites

www.angelfire.com/tx/myquill
Mike Will's comprehensive harmonica site

✍*www.angelfire.com/music/HarpOn*
Chromatic harmonica Web site

✍*www.patmissin.com*
Pat Missin, harmonica player, teacher, technician, and historian is a wealth of information about everything harmonica.

✍*www.spah.org/mc/page.do*
Web site of the Society for the Preservation and Advancement of the Harmonica

APPENDIX C

Glossary

accent To play a beat or note more loudly than the beats or notes surrounding it, thereby emphasizing it.

arpeggio A chord that is played one note at a time in sequential order, either ascending or descending.

articulation syllables Letter sounds like "D" and "T" that you make with your mouth at the beginning of each note to release a concentrated amount of air that produces the hard attack.

attack The way a note begins, from softly to loudly and from smoothly to sharply.

balance The relationship between the volumes of the different instruments playing together.

bar lines The vertical lines that divide measures, also known as "bars," in musical notation.

bass clef Signified by this symbol 𝄢. The lines of the staff, from bottom to top, represent G B D F A.

beat The pulse of a piece of music, usually the note that gets one beat in the time signature.

bending Shifting the pitch of a note either higher or lower.

blow bend An exhale bend that vibrates both reeds simultaneously to produce a bend effect that pulls the note down.

blue notes Changes made to the major scale, specifically a *flatted third* and a *flatted seventh* note, that create harmonic tension between sounds usually identified with a major scale and a minor scale. A *flatted fifth* is also frequently used as an additional blue note.

blues scale A variation of the pentatonic scale that adds a passing tone between the third and fourth notes, creating a 6-note scale. In the key of C, the scale would be C E♭ F F♯ G B♭.

bump bend up A blow bend that begins with the original note, bends it up, and then returns to the original note.

chart This notation has the melody written out on the staff and chord symbols written above the staff, but no lyrics.

chord Three or more notes played at the same time.

chord chart Notation that has only the chord changes of the progression, written as chord symbols, with no melody shown.

chord melodies Created by playing the notes above and below the main melody note to create the chords, forming a sound like a three-part harmony.

chord progression A series of chords that are played to accompany the melody of a song.

chord symbol A way of writing a chord in letter form, rather than as a stack of notes on the staff, such as "Gm7" for a G minor seventh chord.

chorus One time through a chord progression, generally used to define the length, or number of choruses, of a solo.

chromatic A scale with thirteen notes from octave to octave, which includes every possible note in the scale that exists between the two octaves.

circular breathing A breathing technique that allows a musician to play a continuous stream of notes indefinitely.

clef symbol The symbol tells you what notes the lines and spaces of the staff stand for.

comping Short for complementing—playing in a way that supports and encourages a soloist.

consonance A sound where all the notes are in tune with each other and form a stable, pleasant sound.

country scale A variation of the major scale that's often used in country and folk music for its natural bouncy rhythm. It's played by selecting the first, second, third, fifth, sixth, and eighth (octave) notes of the major scale. The scale is also known as a major pentatonic scale.

cross harp Selecting a harp tuned to the key three notes above the key of the song you want to play, and then playing in second position.

delay Making a copy of your original sound and then repeating it after a short delay, hence the name.

diatonic A scale with eight notes from octave to octave, which contains only the notes in the scale of the key being played.

dip bend down A draw bend that begins with the original note, bends it down, and then returns to the original note.

direct box A box that accepts your mic's ¼-inch plug and comes out with a three-pin balanced output jack, used to plug an instrument or microphone directly into a PA system.

dissonance An unstable tonal quality where the combination of notes being played clash with each other and make the listener wish for resolution.

distortion An effect created naturally by overdriving an amplifier to produce a long sustain, or created artificially by using an effects box.

dominant The fifth degree of the scale.

Dorian mode A minor scale that has a flatted third and a flatted seventh (but no flatted sixth as in the natural minor).

dotted note When a dot appears after a note it means that the note is to be played for half again its usual time value. For example, a dot written after a half note, which normally gets two beats in 4/4 time, would now be played for three beats instead.

dotted rest When a dot appears after a rest it means that the rest is to be held for half again its usual time value. For example, a dot written after a half rest, which normally gets held for two beats in 4/4 time, would now be held for three beats instead.

double bend down A draw bend executed twice in rapid succession.

doubling Using two voices to play the same note, phrase, or part.

draw bend An inhale bend that pulls both the draw reed and the blow reed simultaneously, creating a new note that is neither of the reeds' natural tunings. The overall effect of a draw bend is always to pull the pitch of the note down.

draw harp Selecting a harp tuned one note below the key of the song you want to play and then playing in third position.

dynamics How loudly or softly you're playing.

ear training A series of exercises that teach you the skill of listening to a note or phrase and then reproducing it on your instrument.

echo The repeated reproduction of the original sound.

embouchure The manner in which the inside of the mouth is adjusted relative to the mouthpiece of a wind instrument to create various effects.

ensemble playing Playing music with other musicians in a duet or group setting.

fifth position Begins on the 5 blow and enables you to play another type of minor scale known as the Phrygian mode.

first position Playing the major scale that the harmonica is tuned to, usually focusing on holes 4, 5, 6, and 7 blow.

flat sign Looks like this: ♭. When it's written directly in front of a note it means the note is to be lowered one half step below normal.

flatted note A note that's lowered one half step.

fourth position Begins on the 6 draw and enables you to play a natural minor scale in A when played on a C diatonic harmonica.

half-step The smallest space between two notes in Western music.

half-step down bend A draw bend that bends the original note down one half step.

improvisation The spontaneous creation of music in the immediate moment, played without any written music or notation for guidance.

interval Two notes played at the same time.

key signature This appears after the clef symbol in the first measure, and is expressed by one or more sharp signs or flat signs (one type or the other). Because every key has different notes that are always sharp or flat in its scale, these sharps or flats tell you that those notes will always be sharp or flat throughout the entire piece of music, unless otherwise indicated.

lead sheet Also known as sheet music, this notation has the melody line written in notes on the staff, with chord symbols above the staff and the lyrics to the song written below the staff.

major pentatonic A variation of the major scale that's often used in country and folk music for its natural bouncy rhythm. It's played by selecting the first, second, third, fifth, sixth, and eighth (octave) notes of the major scale. The scale is also known as a country scale.

melody A succession of notes assembled to form a purposeful sequence.

metronome A device, either mechanical or electronic, that establishes a steady, reliable beat.

modes Classical scales that grew out of ancient Greek music. They are centered around the notes of a C major scale, and each of the seven modes uses the same consecutive notes of that C major scale—but each mode begins on a different note of that scale.

musical notation Any written system of communicating how to play music.

natural sign Looks like this: ♮. This sign is placed directly in front of a note when a note that's always supposed to be sharp or flat because of the key signature is instead to be played at its original pitch.

octave Two notes with the same letter that are 12 half-steps apart.

overblow An exhale that jams one of the reeds while vibrating the other reed to create an overtone above the original note.

overdrive Pushing a tube amp into saturation by turning the volume up to the maximum to produce a natural distortion.

overtone A separate note created by the vibration caused by playing your original note.

phrase A group of notes that expresses one musical idea.

phrasing The way notes are articulated and assembled into groups. A phrase is a group of notes that expresses a musical thought or idea.

Phrygian mode A minor scale that has a flatted second in addition to a flatted sixth and seventh.

playing by ear The skill of being able to hear a melody, a song, or any piece of music and then being able to play it

polyrhythm Two or more rhythms being played at the same time.

position The location on the harmonica where you begin to play, which is usually where the tonic (first note) of the scale is for the key of the song you're playing.

prebend A bend that begins with the bent note and returns to the original note.

range All of the notes that can be played on an instrument, from the lowest to the highest.

rest sign Symbols that tell you how long you'll be resting (as opposed to playing) within each measure.

regeneration Having more than one echo repeat after your original sound because the output from the delay is being fed back into the input over and over again. This creates the sound of multiple echoes that fade in volume as they repeat.

reverb Short for reverberation, which is the bouncing of sound waves off of many different surfaces in an enclosed space at one time.

riff A series of notes that create a musical idea or phrase.

scale degree The numerical position a note holds in a scale. Every chord has a *root*, a *third*, and a *fifth*.

second position Playing the blues scale in the key a fifth above the key the harmonica is tuned to, focusing on holes 2, 3, 4, 5, and 6 draw.

sharp sign Looks like this: ♯. When it's written directly in front of a note it means that note is to be raised one half step above normal.

sheng A 3,000 year old Chinese instrument considered to be the earliest ancestor of the harmonica.

shuffle A rhythm in 4/4 time where each of the four beats in the measure is divided into triplets. The rhythm is then further refined by accenting just the first and last beat of each group of triplets. It sounds like "shuffle-shuffle-shuffle-shuffle."

slapback The sound of an instrument bouncing once off the back wall of a room, giving your notes a concert-hall quality.

slur Represented by a curved line over or under a group of notes, a group of notes played together smoothly with one note flowing directly into the next, as opposed to each note having a separate hard attack.

staccato To hold a note or chord for as short a duration as possible, like a short burst of sound.

staff The five vertical lines on which standard musical notation is written.

standard notation The most common form of musical notation where all notes and chords are written on a staff of five vertical lines, and all the information you need to play the music—including what key the music is in, what the time signature is, what speed to play it, how loudly or softly to play it, and exactly how long to play each note—is precisely specified.

straight harp Selecting a harp that's in the same key as the song you want to play and then playing the melody in first position.

subdominant The fourth degree of the scale.

syncopation The emphasizing of beats that are normally not the strong or accented beats in the rhythm you're playing.

tablature A form of musical notation that tells you where on your instrument to put your fingers—or in the case of the harmonica, your lips. Because tablature is based on a representation of the physical instrument itself, it is specific to one instrument, so harmonica tablature is completely different from guitar tablature or bagpipe tablature. Besides telling which holes on the harp to use, harmonica tablature, or *tab* for short, tells you whether you should blow or draw that hole, and also whether you should bend the note or not.

tempo The speed at which a piece of music is played.

third An interval of two notes in a scale separated by one note.

third position Playing the minor scale one note above the key the harmonica is tuned to, focusing on holes 4, 5, 6, and 7 draw.

tie Represented by a curved line written between two notes of the same pitch, a tie means you are to hold the note for the total number of beats the two notes are worth together. For example, two half notes (each of which gets two beats) of the same pitch with a tie between them would be played as one note held for four beats.

time signature The third thing that appears in the first measure after the clef symbol and the key signature. Expressed as two numbers, one above the other, the top number tells you how many beats are in each measure, and the bottom number tells you what kind of note gets counted as one beat. For example, in 3/4 time there are three beats per measure and the quarter note gets one beat. In 3/8 time there are three beats per measure and the eighth note gets one beat.

tongue shuffle A technique that combines the techniques of tongue vamping, tongue slapping, octaves, and single notes to create a repeating shuffle rhythm.

tongue slapping A technique that employs basic tongue blocking and adds the action of moving the tongue on and off of the comb to block and unblock holes in order to change the number of notes being played at one time.

tongue vamping A technique that combines the techniques of tongue blocking and tongue slapping to create a repeating rhythmic pattern of alternating single note and chord sounds.

tonic The first note of a scale, and also the first note of the scale of the key the song is in.

treble clef Signified by this symbol 𝄞, the lines of the staff from bottom to top represent E G B D F.

tremolo A sound created by running the volume control of an amplifier through a slow wave form that uniformly raises and lowers the volume at an even pace. This subtle wavering of the volume overlays the sound with a pleasant texture.

triad A three-note chord made up of the first, third, and fifth notes of a scale.

trill Two notes played in rapidly alternating manner.

triplets A rhythm where each individual beat in the measure is divided into three equal parts.

voicing The order in which the notes of a chord are played.

whole-step down bend A draw bend that bends the original note down one whole step.

Index

THE EVERYTHING SERIES!

BUSINESS & PERSONAL FINANCE

Everything® Accounting Book
Everything® Budgeting Book, 2nd Ed.
Everything® Business Planning Book
Everything® Coaching and Mentoring Book, 2nd Ed.
Everything® Fundraising Book
Everything® Get Out of Debt Book
Everything® Grant Writing Book, 2nd Ed.
Everything® Guide to Buying Foreclosures
Everything® Guide to Mortgages
Everything® Guide to Personal Finance for Single Mothers
Everything® Home-Based Business Book, 2nd Ed.
Everything® Homebuying Book, 2nd Ed.
Everything® Homeselling Book, 2nd Ed.
Everything® Human Resource Management Book
Everything® Improve Your Credit Book
Everything® Investing Book, 2nd Ed.
Everything® Landlording Book
Everything® Leadership Book, 2nd Ed.
Everything® Managing People Book, 2nd Ed.
Everything® Negotiating Book
Everything® Online Auctions Book
Everything® Online Business Book
Everything® Personal Finance Book
Everything® Personal Finance in Your 20s & 30s Book, 2nd Ed.
Everything® Project Management Book, 2nd Ed.
Everything® Real Estate Investing Book
Everything® Retirement Planning Book
Everything® Robert's Rules Book, $7.95
Everything® Selling Book
Everything® Start Your Own Business Book, 2nd Ed.
Everything® Wills & Estate Planning Book

COOKING

Everything® Barbecue Cookbook
Everything® Bartender's Book, 2nd Ed., $9.95
Everything® Calorie Counting Cookbook
Everything® Cheese Book
Everything® Chinese Cookbook
Everything® Classic Recipes Book
Everything® Cocktail Parties & Drinks Book
Everything® College Cookbook
Everything® Cooking for Baby and Toddler Book
Everything® Cooking for Two Cookbook
Everything® Diabetes Cookbook
Everything® Easy Gourmet Cookbook
Everything® Fondue Cookbook
Everything® Fondue Party Book
Everything® Gluten-Free Cookbook
Everything® Glycemic Index Cookbook
Everything® Grilling Cookbook
Everything® Healthy Meals in Minutes Cookbook
Everything® Holiday Cookbook
Everything® Indian Cookbook
Everything® Italian Cookbook

Everything® Lactose-Free Cookbook
Everything® Low-Carb Cookbook
Everything® Low-Cholesterol Cookbook
Everything® Low-Fat High-Flavor Cookbook
Everything® Low-Salt Cookbook
Everything® Meals for a Month Cookbook
Everything® Meals on a Budget Cookbook
Everything® Mediterranean Cookbook
Everything® Mexican Cookbook
Everything® No Trans Fat Cookbook
Everything® One-Pot Cookbook
Everything® Pizza Cookbook
Everything® Quick and Easy 30-Minute,
    5-Ingredient Cookbook
Everything® Quick Meals Cookbook
Everything® Slow Cooker Cookbook
Everything® Slow Cooking for a Crowd Cookbook
Everything® Soup Cookbook
Everything® Stir-Fry Cookbook
Everything® Sugar-Free Cookbook
Everything® Tapas and Small Plates Cookbook
Everything® Tex-Mex Cookbook
Everything® Thai Cookbook
Everything® Vegetarian Cookbook
Everything® Whole-Grain, High-Fiber Cookbook
Everything® Wild Game Cookbook
Everything® Wine Book, 2nd Ed.

GAMES

Everything® 15-Minute Sudoku Book, $9.95
Everything® 30-Minute Sudoku Book, $9.95
Everything® Bible Crosswords Book, $9.95
Everything® Blackjack Strategy Book
Everything® Brain Strain Book, $9.95
Everything® Bridge Book
Everything® Card Games Book
Everything® Card Tricks Book, $9.95
Everything® Casino Gambling Book, 2nd Ed.
Everything® Chess Basics Book
Everything® Craps Strategy Book
Everything® Crossword and Puzzle Book
Everything® Crossword Challenge Book
Everything® Crosswords for the Beach Book, $9.95
Everything® Cryptic Crosswords Book, $9.95
Everything® Cryptograms Book, $9.95
Everything® Easy Crosswords Book
Everything® Easy Kakuro Book, $9.95
Everything® Easy Large-Print Crosswords Book
Everything® Games Book, 2nd Ed.
Everything® Giant Sudoku Book, $9.95
Everything® Giant Word Search Book
Everything® Kakuro Challenge Book, $9.95
Everything® Large-Print Crossword Challenge Book
Everything® Large-Print Crosswords Book
Everything® Lateral Thinking Puzzles Book, $9.95
Everything® Literary Crosswords Book, $9.95
Everything® Mazes Book
Everything® Memory Booster Puzzles Book, $9.95
Everything® Movie Crosswords Book, $9.95

Everything® Music Crosswords Book, $9.95
Everything® Online Poker Book
Everything® Pencil Puzzles Book, $9.95
Everything® Poker Strategy Book
Everything® Pool & Billiards Book
Everything® Puzzles for Commuters Book, $9.95
Everything® Puzzles for Dog Lovers Book, $9.95
Everything® Sports Crosswords Book, $9.95
Everything® Test Your IQ Book, $9.95
Everything® Texas Hold 'Em Book, $9.95
Everything® Travel Crosswords Book, $9.95
Everything® TV Crosswords Book, $9.95
Everything® Word Games Challenge Book
Everything® Word Scramble Book
Everything® Word Search Book

HEALTH

Everything® Alzheimer's Book
Everything® Diabetes Book
Everything® First Aid Book, $9.95
Everything® Health Guide to Adult Bipolar Disorder
Everything® Health Guide to Arthritis
Everything® Health Guide to Controlling Anxiety
Everything® Health Guide to Depression
Everything® Health Guide to Fibromyalgia
Everything® Health Guide to Menopause, 2nd Ed.
Everything® Health Guide to Migraines
Everything® Health Guide to OCD
Everything® Health Guide to PMS
Everything® Health Guide to Postpartum Care
Everything® Health Guide to Thyroid Disease
Everything® Hypnosis Book
Everything® Low Cholesterol Book
Everything® Menopause Book
Everything® Nutrition Book
Everything® Reflexology Book
Everything® Stress Management Book

HISTORY

Everything® American Government Book
Everything® American History Book, 2nd Ed.
Everything® Civil War Book
Everything® Freemasons Book
Everything® Irish History & Heritage Book
Everything® Middle East Book
Everything® World War II Book, 2nd Ed.

HOBBIES

Everything® Candlemaking Book
Everything® Cartooning Book
Everything® Coin Collecting Book
Everything® Digital Photography Book, 2nd Ed.
Everything® Drawing Book
Everything® Family Tree Book, 2nd Ed.
Everything® Knitting Book
Everything® Knots Book
Everything® Photography Book
Everything® Quilting Book

Everything® Sewing Book
Everything® Soapmaking Book, 2nd Ed.
Everything® Woodworking Book

HOME IMPROVEMENT

Everything® Feng Shui Book
Everything® Feng Shui Decluttering Book, $9.95
Everything® Fix-It Book
Everything® Green Living Book
Everything® Home Decorating Book
Everything® Home Storage Solutions Book
Everything® Homebuilding Book
Everything® Organize Your Home Book, 2nd Ed.

KIDS' BOOKS

All titles are $7.95
Everything® Fairy Tales Book, $14.95
Everything® Kids' Animal Puzzle & Activity Book
Everything® Kids' Astronomy Book
Everything® Kids' Baseball Book, 5th Ed.
Everything® Kids' Bible Trivia Book
Everything® Kids' Bugs Book
Everything® Kids' Cars and Trucks Puzzle and Activity Book
Everything® Kids' Christmas Puzzle & Activity Book
Everything® Kids' Connect the Dots
Puzzle and Activity Book
Everything® Kids' Cookbook
Everything® Kids' Crazy Puzzles Book
Everything® Kids' Dinosaurs Book
Everything® Kids' Environment Book
Everything® Kids' Fairies Puzzle and Activity Book
Everything® Kids' First Spanish Puzzle and Activity Book
Everything® Kids' Football Book
Everything® Kids' Gross Cookbook
Everything® Kids' Gross Hidden Pictures Book
Everything® Kids' Gross Jokes Book
Everything® Kids' Gross Mazes Book
Everything® Kids' Gross Puzzle & Activity Book
Everything® Kids' Halloween Puzzle & Activity Book
Everything® Kids' Hidden Pictures Book
Everything® Kids' Horses Book
Everything® Kids' Joke Book
Everything® Kids' Knock Knock Book
Everything® Kids' Learning French Book
Everything® Kids' Learning Spanish Book
Everything® Kids' Magical Science Experiments Book
Everything® Kids' Math Puzzles Book
Everything® Kids' Mazes Book
Everything® Kids' Money Book
Everything® Kids' Nature Book
Everything® Kids' Pirates Puzzle and Activity Book
Everything® Kids' Presidents Book
Everything® Kids' Princess Puzzle and Activity Book
Everything® Kids' Puzzle Book
Everything® Kids' Racecars Puzzle and Activity Book
Everything® Kids' Riddles & Brain Teasers Book
Everything® Kids' Science Experiments Book
Everything® Kids' Sharks Book
Everything® Kids' Soccer Book
Everything® Kids' Spies Puzzle and Activity Book
Everything® Kids' States Book
Everything® Kids' Travel Activity Book
Everything® Kids' Word Search Puzzle and Activity Book

LANGUAGE

Everything® Conversational Japanese Book with CD, $19.95
Everything® French Grammar Book
Everything® French Phrase Book, $9.95
Everything® French Verb Book, $9.95
Everything® German Practice Book with CD, $19.95
Everything® Inglés Book
Everything® Intermediate Spanish Book with CD, $19.95
Everything® Italian Practice Book with CD, $19.95
Everything® Learning Brazilian Portuguese Book with CD, $19.95
Everything® Learning French Book with CD, 2nd Ed., $19.95
Everything® Learning German Book
Everything® Learning Italian Book
Everything® Learning Latin Book
Everything® Learning Russian Book with CD, $19.95
Everything® Learning Spanish Book
Everything® Learning Spanish Book with CD, 2nd Ed., $19.95
Everything® Russian Practice Book with CD, $19.95
Everything® Sign Language Book
Everything® Spanish Grammar Book
Everything® Spanish Phrase Book, $9.95
Everything® Spanish Practice Book with CD, $19.95
Everything® Spanish Verb Book, $9.95
Everything® Speaking Mandarin Chinese Book with CD, $19.95

MUSIC

Everything® Bass Guitar Book with CD, $19.95
Everything® Drums Book with CD, $19.95
Everything® Guitar Book with CD, 2nd Ed., $19.95
Everything® Guitar Chords Book with CD, $19.95
Everything® Harmonica Book with CD, $15.95
Everything® Home Recording Book
Everything® Music Theory Book with CD, $19.95
Everything® Reading Music Book with CD, $19.95
Everything® Rock & Blues Guitar Book with CD, $19.95
Everything® Rock & Blues Piano Book with CD, $19.95
Everything® Songwriting Book

NEW AGE

Everything® Astrology Book, 2nd Ed.
Everything® Birthday Personology Book
Everything® Dreams Book, 2nd Ed.
Everything® Love Signs Book, $9.95
Everything® Love Spells Book, $9.95
Everything® Paganism Book
Everything® Palmistry Book
Everything® Psychic Book
Everything® Reiki Book
Everything® Sex Signs Book, $9.95
Everything® Spells & Charms Book, 2nd Ed.
Everything® Tarot Book, 2nd Ed.
Everything® Toltec Wisdom Book
Everything® Wicca & Witchcraft Book, 2nd Ed.

PARENTING

Everything® Baby Names Book, 2nd Ed.
Everything® Baby Shower Book, 2nd Ed.
Everything® Baby Sign Language Book with DVD
Everything® Baby's First Year Book
Everything® Birthing Book

Everything® Breastfeeding Book
Everything® Father-to-Be Book
Everything® Father's First Year Book
Everything® Get Ready for Baby Book, 2nd Ed.
Everything® Get Your Baby to Sleep Book, $9.95
Everything® Getting Pregnant Book
Everything® Guide to Pregnancy Over 35
Everything® Guide to Raising a One-Year-Old
Everything® Guide to Raising a Two-Year-Old
Everything® Guide to Raising Adolescent Boys
Everything® Guide to Raising Adolescent Girls
Everything® Mother's First Year Book
Everything® Parent's Guide to Childhood Illnesses
Everything® Parent's Guide to Children and Divorce
Everything® Parent's Guide to Children with ADD/ADHD
Everything® Parent's Guide to Children with Asperger's Syndrome
Everything® Parent's Guide to Children with Asthma
Everything® Parent's Guide to Children with Autism
Everything® Parent's Guide to Children with Bipolar Disorder
Everything® Parent's Guide to Children with Depression
Everything® Parent's Guide to Children with Dyslexia
Everything® Parent's Guide to Children with Juvenile Diabetes
Everything® Parent's Guide to Positive Discipline
Everything® Parent's Guide to Raising a Successful Child
Everything® Parent's Guide to Raising Boys
Everything® Parent's Guide to Raising Girls
Everything® Parent's Guide to Raising Siblings
Everything® Parent's Guide to Sensory Integration Disorder
Everything® Parent's Guide to Tantrums
Everything® Parent's Guide to the Strong-Willed Child
Everything® Parenting a Teenager Book
Everything® Potty Training Book, $9.95
Everything® Pregnancy Book, 3rd Ed.
Everything® Pregnancy Fitness Book
Everything® Pregnancy Nutrition Book
Everything® Pregnancy Organizer, 2nd Ed., $16.95
Everything® Toddler Activities Book
Everything® Toddler Book
Everything® Tween Book
Everything® Twins, Triplets, and More Book

PETS

Everything® Aquarium Book
Everything® Boxer Book
Everything® Cat Book, 2nd Ed.
Everything® Chihuahua Book
Everything® Cooking for Dogs Book
Everything® Dachshund Book
Everything® Dog Book, 2nd Ed.
Everything® Dog Grooming Book
Everything® Dog Health Book
Everything® Dog Obedience Book
Everything® Dog Owner's Organizer, $16.95
Everything® Dog Training and Tricks Book
Everything® German Shepherd Book
Everything® Golden Retriever Book
Everything® Horse Book
Everything® Horse Care Book
Everything® Horseback Riding Book
Everything® Labrador Retriever Book
Everything® Poodle Book
Everything® Pug Book

Everything® Puppy Book
Everything® Rottweiler Book
Everything® Small Dogs Book
Everything® Tropical Fish Book
Everything® Yorkshire Terrier Book

REFERENCE

Everything® American Presidents Book
Everything® Blogging Book
Everything® Build Your Vocabulary Book, $9.95
Everything® Car Care Book
Everything® Classical Mythology Book
Everything® Da Vinci Book
Everything® Divorce Book
Everything® Einstein Book
Everything® Enneagram Book
Everything® Etiquette Book, 2nd Ed.
Everything® Guide to C. S. Lewis & Narnia
Everything® Guide to Edgar Allan Poe
Everything® Guide to Understanding Philosophy
Everything® Inventions and Patents Book
Everything® Jacqueline Kennedy Onassis Book
Everything® John F. Kennedy Book
Everything® Mafia Book
Everything® Martin Luther King Jr. Book
Everything® Philosophy Book
Everything® Pirates Book
Everything® Private Investigation Book
Everything® Psychology Book
Everything® Public Speaking Book, $9.95
Everything® Shakespeare Book, 2nd Ed.

RELIGION

Everything® Angels Book
Everything® Bible Book
Everything® Bible Study Book with CD, $19.95
Everything® Buddhism Book
Everything® Catholicism Book
Everything® Christianity Book
Everything® Gnostic Gospels Book
Everything® History of the Bible Book
Everything® Jesus Book
Everything® Jewish History & Heritage Book
Everything® Judaism Book
Everything® Kabbalah Book
Everything® Koran Book
Everything® Mary Book
Everything® Mary Magdalene Book
Everything® Prayer Book
Everything® Saints Book, 2nd Ed.
Everything® Torah Book
Everything® Understanding Islam Book
Everything® Women of the Bible Book
Everything® World's Religions Book

SCHOOL & CAREERS

Everything® Career Tests Book
Everything® College Major Test Book
Everything® College Survival Book, 2nd Ed.
Everything® Cover Letter Book, 2nd Ed.
Everything® Filmmaking Book
Everything® Get-a-Job Book, 2nd Ed.
Everything® Guide to Being a Paralegal
Everything® Guide to Being a Personal Trainer
Everything® Guide to Being a Real Estate Agent
Everything® Guide to Being a Sales Rep
Everything® Guide to Being an Event Planner
Everything® Guide to Careers in Health Care
Everything® Guide to Careers in Law Enforcement
Everything® Guide to Government Jobs
Everything® Guide to Starting and Running a Catering
   Business
Everything® Guide to Starting and Running a Restaurant
Everything® Job Interview Book, 2nd Ed.
Everything® New Nurse Book
Everything® New Teacher Book
Everything® Paying for College Book
Everything® Practice Interview Book
Everything® Resume Book, 3rd Ed.
Everything® Study Book

SELF-HELP

Everything® Body Language Book
Everything® Dating Book, 2nd Ed.
Everything® Great Sex Book
Everything® Self-Esteem Book
Everything® Tantric Sex Book

SPORTS & FITNESS

Everything® Easy Fitness Book
Everything® Fishing Book
Everything® Krav Maga for Fitness Book
Everything® Running Book, 2nd Ed.

TRAVEL

Everything® Family Guide to Coastal Florida
Everything® Family Guide to Cruise Vacations
Everything® Family Guide to Hawaii
Everything® Family Guide to Las Vegas, 2nd Ed.
Everything® Family Guide to Mexico
Everything® Family Guide to New England, 2nd Ed.
Everything® Family Guide to New York City, 3rd Ed.
Everything® Family Guide to RV Travel & Campgrounds
Everything® Family Guide to the Caribbean
Everything® Family Guide to the Disneyland® Resort, California
   Adventure®, Universal Studios®, and the Anaheim
   Area, 2nd Ed.
Everything® Family Guide to the Walt Disney World Resort®,
   Universal Studios®, and Greater Orlando, 5th Ed.
Everything® Family Guide to Timeshares
Everything® Family Guide to Washington D.C., 2nd Ed.

WEDDINGS

Everything® Bachelorette Party Book, $9.95
Everything® Bridesmaid Book, $9.95
Everything® Destination Wedding Book
Everything® Father of the Bride Book, $9.95
Everything® Groom Book, $9.95
Everything® Mother of the Bride Book, $9.95
Everything® Outdoor Wedding Book
Everything® Wedding Book, 3rd Ed.
Everything® Wedding Checklist, $9.95
Everything® Wedding Etiquette Book, $9.95
Everything® Wedding Organizer, 2nd Ed., $16.95
Everything® Wedding Shower Book, $9.95
Everything® Wedding Vows Book, $9.95
Everything® Wedding Workout Book
Everything® Weddings on a Budget Book, 2nd Ed., $9.95

WRITING

Everything® Creative Writing Book
Everything® Get Published Book, 2nd Ed.
Everything® Grammar and Style Book, 2nd Ed.
Everything® Guide to Magazine Writing
Everything® Guide to Writing a Book Proposal
Everything® Guide to Writing a Novel
Everything® Guide to Writing Children's Books
Everything® Guide to Writing Copy
Everything® Guide to Writing Graphic Novels
Everything® Guide to Writing Research Papers
Everything® Improve Your Writing Book, 2nd Ed.
Everything® Writing Poetry Book